WHAT SMALL GROUP LEADERS AND MEMBERS ARE EXPERIENCING CHR

My group was formed four years ago of very new believers. EXPERIENCING CHRIST TOGETHER has helped form bonds, and we have fallen in love with Christ. We have had many trials, but we have learned to lean on the body of Christ to carry us through the difficult times. I know our lives are richer than ever.

—Leader

The EXPERIENCING CHRIST TOGETHER series has motivated me more than any other Bible study that I have ever been to. This Bible study gets to the heart of the matter—my character in Christ—and that has created action on my part.

—Leader

I love the fact that Jesus' life shows us how to live.

—Member

This series is an "awakening." Jesus has become a very personal friend.

—Leader

This series is definitely a must-do as the foundation for a healthy, maturing small group!

—Leader

EXPERIENCING CHRIST TOGETHER is a safe place to learn about the living Jesus and how he wants to lead us and love us.

—Member

EXPERIENCING CHRIST TOGETHER ties the heart and the mind together. The Bible knowledge grows the mind and the life application grows the heart and transforms the soul.

—Member

Other Studies in the EXPERIENCING CHRIST TOGETHER Series

Beginning in Christ Together (Life of Jesus)

Connecting in Christ Together (Fellowship)

Serving Like Christ Together (Ministry)

Sharing Christ Together (Evangelism)

Surrendering to Christ Together (Worship)

Studies in the DOING LIFE TOGETHER Series

Beginning Life Together (God's Purpose for Your Life)

Connecting with God's Family (Fellowship)

Growing to Be Like Christ (Discipleship)

Developing Your SHAPE to Serve Others (Ministry)

Sharing Your Life Mission Every Day (Evangelism)

Surrendering Your Life to God's Pleasure (Worship)

GROWING IN CHRIST TOGETHER

six sessions on
Discipleship

written by
BRETT and **DEE EASTMAN**
TODD and **DENISE WENDORFF**
KAREN LEE-THORP

GRAND RAPIDS, MICHIGAN 49530 USA

ZONDERVAN™

Growing in Christ Together
Copyright © 2005 by Brett and Deanna Eastman, Todd and Denise Wendorff,
and Karen Lee-Thorp

Requests for information should be addressed to:

Zondervan, *Grand Rapids, Michigan 49530*

ISBN 0-310-24985-6

Interior icons by Tom Clark

Interior design by Beth Shagene & Michelle Espinoza

Printed in the United States of America

05 06 07 08 09 10 11 /❖ DCI/ 10 9 8 7 6 5 4 3 2

CONTENTS

Read Me First   7

SESSION 1   The Treasure of Discipleship   13
SESSION 2   The Power of the Desert   24
            Personal Health Plan   34
SESSION 3   Pressing the Pause Button   36
SESSION 4   Persistent Prayer   45
SESSION 5   Building on a Solid Foundation   54
SESSION 6   Where's Your Treasure?   62

APPENDIX
            Frequently Asked Questions   71
            LIFE TOGETHER Agreement   74
            Small Group Calendar   76
            Team Roles   77
            Personal Health Assessment   80
            Personal Health Plan   82
            Sample Personal Health Plan   84
            Journaling 101   86
            Bible Reading Plan: 30 Days   87
                through the Gospel of John
            Leading for the First Time   89
            Hosting an Open House   91
            EXPERIENCING CHRIST TOGETHER   92
                in a Sunday School Setting
            A Simple Retreat Plan   94

LEADER'S NOTES   97

About the Authors   111
Small Group Roster   112

EXPERIENCING CHRIST TOGETHER

EXPERIENCING CHRIST TOGETHER: LIVING WITH PURPOSE IN COMMUNITY will take you face to face with Jesus himself. In addition to being the Son of God and Savior of the world, Jesus holds the greatest wisdom and understands the purposes for which God formed you. He knows what it takes to build authentic relationships, to know God more intensely, to grow spiritually, and ultimately to make a difference in the world. EXPERIENCING CHRIST TOGETHER offers you a chance to do what Jesus' first followers did: spend time with him, listen to what he said, watch what he did, and pattern your life after his.

Jesus lived every moment following God's purpose for his life. In this study you will experience firsthand how he did this and how you can do it too. Yet if you're anything like us, knowing what God wants for you is one thing, but doing it is something else. That's why you'll follow Jesus' plan of doing life not alone but together. As you follow in his footsteps, you'll find his pathway more exciting than anything you've imagined.

Book 1 of this series (*Beginning in Christ Together*) explores the person of Jesus Christ. Each of the subsequent five studies looks through Jesus' eyes at one of God's five biblical purposes for his people (fellowship, discipleship, service, evangelism, and worship). For example, *Growing in Christ Together* deals with discipleship. Book 1 is about grace: what Christ has done for us. The other books (including this one) are about how we live in response to grace.

Even if you've done another LIFE TOGETHER study, you'll be amazed at how Jesus can take you to places of faith you've never been before. The joy of life in him is far beyond a life you could design on your own. If you do all six study guides in this series, you'll spend one astonishing year with Jesus Christ.

Becoming Like Christ

In ancient times, a young man who wanted to learn a trade would apprentice himself to a master. The apprentice would work alongside the master, watching what he did and following his instructions. As the apprentice's skills improved, the master would give him more responsibilities.

The same was true in spiritual matters. If a Jew wanted to learn how to live in a way that pleased God, he would apprentice himself to a master, called a rabbi or teacher. The apprentice was called a disciple.

Jesus was the most remarkable rabbi of his day. He is also the most remarkable rabbi of our day, for he's still alive. He has the most wisdom about how to live the abundant, fruitful life God intends for us. If we're willing to be his apprentices, we can learn to do life the way Jesus would if he had our temperaments, our families, and our jobs.

Part of our apprenticeship involves habits that Jesus himself cultivated, such as deliberately resisting the frenzied pace of life. How can we possibly do that in our complex world? *Growing in Christ Together* shows us how to do this and more. We'll learn to see the Father through Jesus' eyes when we pray, and how Jesus chose the priorities of his life. If we want to walk intimately with the Father, able to handle whatever the world throws at us, Jesus is eager to teach us.

Outline of Each Session

Most people want to live healthy, balanced spiritual lives, but few achieve this alone. And most small groups struggle to balance all of God's purposes in their meetings. Groups tend to overemphasize one of the five purposes, perhaps fellowship or discipleship. Rarely is there a healthy balance that includes evangelism, ministry, and worship. That's why we've included all of these elements in this study so you can live a healthy, balanced spiritual life over time.

A typical group session will include the following:

 CONNECTING WITH GOD'S FAMILY (FELLOWSHIP). The foundation for spiritual growth is an intimate connection with God and his family. A few people who really know you and who earn your trust provide a place to experience the life Jesus invites you to live. This section of each session typically offers you two options. You can get to know your whole group by using the icebreaker question (always question 1), or you can check in with one or two group members— your spiritual partner(s)—for a deeper connection and encouragement in your spiritual journey.

DVD TEACHING SEGMENT. A DVD companion to this study guide is available. For each study session, a teacher discusses the topic, ordinary Christians talk about the personal experience of the topic, a scholar gives background on the Bible passage, and a leadership coach gives tips to the group leader. The DVD contains worship helps and other features as well. If you are using the DVD, you will view the teaching segment after your Connecting discussion and before your Bible study (the Growing section). At the end of each session in this study guide you will find space for your notes on the teaching segment. To view a sample of the DVD, log on to www.lifetogether.com/ ExperiencingChristTogether.

 GROWING TO BE LIKE CHRIST (DISCIPLESHIP). Here is where you come face to face with Christ. In a core Bible passage you'll see Jesus in action, teaching or demonstrating some aspect of how he wants you to live. The focus won't be on accumulating information but on how Jesus' words and actions relate to what you say and do. We want to help you apply the Scriptures practically, creatively, and from your heart as well as your head. At the end of the day, allowing the timeless truths from God's Word to transform our lives in Christ is our greatest aim.

FOR DEEPER STUDY. If you want to dig deeper into more Bible passages about the topic at hand, we've provided additional passages and questions. Your group may choose to do study homework ahead of each meeting in order to cover more biblical material. Or you as an individual may choose to study the For Deeper Study passages on your own. If you prefer not to do study homework, the Growing section will provide you with plenty to discuss within the group. These options allow individuals or the whole group to go deeper in their study, while still accommodating those who can't do homework or are new to your group.

You can record your discoveries on the Reflections page at the end of each session. We encourage you to read some of your insights to a friend (spiritual partner) for accountability and support. Spiritual partners may check in each week over the phone, through email, or at the beginning of the group meeting.

DEVELOPING YOUR GIFTS TO SERVE OTHERS (MINISTRY). Jesus trained his disciples to discover and develop their gifts to serve others. God has designed you uniquely to serve him in a way no other person can. This section will help you discover and use your God-given design. It will also encourage your group to discover your unique design as a community. In two sessions in this study, you'll put into practice what you've learned in the Bible study by taking a step to serve others. These simple steps will take your group on a faith journey that could change your lives forever.

SHARING YOUR LIFE MISSION EVERY DAY (EVANGELISM). Many people skip over this aspect of the Christian life because it's scary, relationally awkward, or simply too much work for their busy schedules. But Jesus wanted all of his disciples to help outsiders connect with him, to know him personally. This doesn't mean preaching on street corners. It could mean welcoming a few newcomers into your group, hosting a short-term group in your home, participating in a cross-cultural missions project, or walking through this study with a friend. In four sessions of this study, you'll have an opportunity to take a small step in this area. These steps will take you beyond Bible study to Bible living.

SURRENDERING YOUR LIFE FOR GOD'S PLEASURE (WORSHIP). God is most pleased by a heart that is fully his. Each group session will give you a chance to surrender your heart to God in prayer and worship. You may read a psalm together, share a page in your journal, or use one of the songs on the DVD to open or close your meeting. (Additional music is available on the LIFE TOGETHER Worship DVD/CD series, produced by Maranatha!) If you've never prayed aloud in a group before, no one will put pressure on you. Instead, you'll experience the support of others who are praying for you. This time will knit your hearts in community and help you surrender all your hurts and dreams into the hands of the One who knows you best.

STUDY NOTES. This section provides background notes on the Bible passage(s) you examine in the Growing section. You may want to refer to these notes during your group meeting or as a reference for those doing additional study.

REFLECTIONS. At the end of each session is a blank page on which you can write your insights from your personal time with God.

Whether you do deeper Bible study, read through the Gospels, meditate on a few verses, or simply write out your prayers, you'll benefit from writing down what you discover. You may want to pick up a blank journal or notepad after you fill in these pages.

SESSION 1
THE TREASURE OF DISCIPLESHIP

Karen and Cindy both have families and full-time jobs. With people and tasks constantly demanding attention, the two women could easily ignore their spiritual lives other than church attendance. But Karen and Cindy are committed to helping each other grow in Christlikeness. So for six years they've met weekly—in person or on the phone—to talk frankly about their lives and to pray. Each week brings reasons why they don't have time: the drive is so long; they're tired after a busy day; there are errands to run and laundry to wash. But each week when they finish praying, they're grateful they made the time. Their partnership is costly, but the benefits far outweigh the costs.

For example, Karen has chosen Ephesians 4:29 as the prayer focus for her relationship with her stepdaughters, so she and Cindy are asking God to give her words that build up and impart grace to her girls. Both women are convinced that they are more loving, joyful, and faith-filled than they would be if they weren't making their spiritual partnership a priority.

Much has been written about the cost of discipleship, the price of pursuing spiritual growth. It's important for you to count the cost, but it's just as important to know the *value* of what you get in return. In this session you'll look at the value of what Christ offers you and decide how much you think it's worth.

CONNECTING WITH GOD'S FAMILY   20 min.

Christ loves you just the way you are. Spiritual growth won't earn you any more of his love. But Christ also has a vision for who you can become: more peaceful as you trust him in stressful circumstances, more loving toward the difficult people in your life, more able to overcome your bad habits. Question 1 invites you to think about the person you are now: a package of strengths and weaknesses. Don't be embarrassed to say something good about yourself!

13

1. What is one thing you like about who you are today? What is one thing about yourself you'd like to change?

2. Whether your group is brand new or ongoing, it's always important to reflect on and review your values together. On pages 74–75 is a sample agreement with the values we've found most useful in sustaining healthy, balanced groups. We recommend that you choose one or two values—ones you haven't previously focused on or have room to grow in—to emphasize during this study. Choose ones that will take your group to the next stage of intimacy and spiritual health.

   ☐ *For new groups:* You may want to focus on encouraging each other's growth. If you don't already have spiritual partners, this is a great time to start. You'll learn more about spiritual partners in session 2.

   ☐ *For existing groups:* We recommend that you rotate host homes on a regular basis and let the hosts lead the meeting. We've come to realize that healthy groups rotate leadership. This helps to develop every member's ability to shepherd a few people in a safe environment. Even Jesus gave others the opportunity to serve alongside him (Mark 6:30–44). Session 3 will explain how to set up a rotating schedule.

GROWING TO BE LIKE CHRIST   30 min.

To be a disciple of Jesus is to let the Holy Spirit train and transform us to do life as he did. We are learning to live in a realm Jesus called "the kingdom of heaven"—the realm where everyone lives as God intended.

Of course, God will welcome us after we die based on our faith in his Son even if we rarely pray and never crack the cover of our Bibles. If that's the case, we might ask, then why bother learning to live the way Jesus would have us live? It certainly isn't the path of least resistance.

The cost of discipleship is high. But Jesus offers a vision for the *value* of discipleship. He knows we will never stay on the path unless we are passionate about the destination. We need a vision of who we can become, of what life in God's kingdom can be like.

3. Read Matthew 13:44. How is God's kingdom like a treasure?

4. On page 20, read the study note on "the kingdom of heaven." What, if anything, surprises you about this information?

5. The man in Jesus' story pays an enormous cost to get the treasure. If God's gift of salvation is free, why does Jesus portray God's kingdom as costly?

6. The man in the story feels joy, even though he pays a huge price. Why should we be thrilled if we have to sell everything to get God's kingdom?

7. What are the benefits of living in a kingdom where things are done God's way rather than our way?

8. Life in God's kingdom today is available only to Jesus' disciples. Read Luke 9:23–27. According to this passage:

What are the costs of discipleship? (You may want to consult this passage in the Study Notes.)

What are the costs of non-discipleship?

9. What costs of following Jesus have been hardest for you to pay?

10. Do you tend to be more troubled by the costs of following Jesus or more joyful about the benefits? Why do you think that is the case?

11. On the next page are some possible steps you could take to let Jesus become your "personal trainer." Which of them are you willing to take for the next six weeks?

☐ *Prayer.* Set aside some time to pray about letting Jesus train you in how to live. You might try just five minutes a day when you get up in the morning or when you arrive at work. You could pray, "Jesus, train me to live today. Train me to think your thoughts. Train me to do what you would do." Then review your day with him. You may find it helpful to write your prayer in a notebook or on the Reflections page near the end of this chapter.

☐ *Bible Reading.* On pages 87–88 is a plan for reading through the gospel of John in thirty days. We recommend that you jot down your thoughts on the Reflections page or in a journal.

☐ *Meditation.* If you've done a lot of Bible study before, try meditation as a way of internalizing God's Word more deeply. Several alternative verses for meditation are suggested on the Reflections page. Copy the verse onto a card, and tape it somewhere in your line of sight, such as your car's dashboard or the kitchen table. Think about it when you sit at red lights, or while you're eating a meal. What is God saying to you, here and now, through these words? On the Reflections page, write a prayer to God about this passage.

FOR DEEPER STUDY

Read Romans 8:5–6; 14:17. How much is a kingdom of life, peace, righteousness, and joy worth to you?

Why is it necessary to count the cost of following Jesus (Luke 14:25–35)? What has it already cost you to follow Jesus, and what might it cost you in the future?

What do you think Jesus means in Luke 14:26 when he says we need to hate our families compared to the value we place on him (see also Matthew 10:37–39)?

SHARING YOUR LIFE MISSION EVERY DAY   10 min.

12. Spiritual growth has an outward dimension as well as an inward one. Jesus wants you to develop the kind of compassion for people that he has. Who are the people in your life who need a group like yours to help them meet Jesus or grow deeper in their faith? The "Circles of Life" diagram on the following page will help you think of people in various areas of your life. Prayerfully write down at least three or four names in the circles.

☐ Which of the people you named can you invite to join your group?

☐ Is there someone you wouldn't invite to your group but who still needs spiritual nourishment and encouragement? Would you be willing to have lunch or coffee with that person, catch up on his or her life, and share something you've learned from this study? You could even do each session of this study with your friend one week after you do it with the group. You won't believe how much more you'll grow if you give away what you've learned each week. Jesus doesn't call all of us to lead small groups, but he does call every disciple to help others grow.

CIRCLES OF LIFE

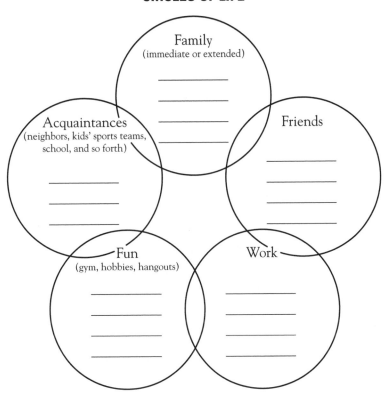

 SURRENDERING YOUR LIFE FOR GOD'S PLEASURE   15–30 min.

13. Gather into circles of three or four people. As you think about the costs of discipleship, it's helpful to remind yourselves of the value of the treasure you've already received from God. Share with your circle one thing God has done for you that you're thankful for.

14. Now share with your circle one thing you'd like to ask God to do. Write down each person's prayer requests in the Prayer and Praise Report on page 21.

15. Pray for each other in your circle. Anyone who isn't used to praying aloud should feel free to offer prayers in silence. Or, if you're new to prayer and you're feeling brave, try praying just one sentence, "God, please help me to _____."

STUDY NOTES

Jesus' stories, like the one in Matthew 13:44, are called parables. They're meant to jar you into seeing the world in a new way and then taking action.

The kingdom of heaven (Matthew 13:44). We often think of heaven as far away and simply the place where we'll go when we die. Angels and clouds and harps come to mind. But that's not what Jesus meant when he talked about the kingdom of heaven. He said, "The kingdom of heaven is near" (Matthew 4:17). It's not far away, and it's not just after you die. It's near. It's now.

The kingdom is the realm where creation, humans, and other creatures do what God wants done, not just because they should (out of fear), but because they want to (out of joy). See, for example, Psalm 19:1–3. Jesus' teaching reveals to all disciples precisely what kingdom living looks like. God invites you to become one of these joyful ones not just after you die, but starting today, and more and more each day into eternity.

Bought (13:44). In the parable, buying the field is a figure of speech. Jesus knows we don't buy our way into God's kingdom. The kingdom is God's gift to us; we receive it by faith (Romans 4:1–5; Ephesians 2:8–9). And it's the Holy Spirit's job to transform us into people who enjoy doing what God wants done. Buying the field is Jesus' way of pointing to the cost of cooperating with the Holy Spirit and the cost of doing things God's way rather than our way.

Take up his cross daily (Luke 9:23). Roman law declared that a prisoner sentenced to the cross gave up all rights as a citizen and became owned completely by the state. Similarly, we give up all rights when we come to Christ as a disciple. We belong to God, who has bought us at the price of Jesus' blood (1 Corinthians 6:19–20; Romans 6:16–18). We give God the right to decide which of our needs and desires he will meet, and when and how he will do so. Entrusting our deepest needs and desires to God often feels like death. The "me" we thought we were dies so that the "me" God created can fully live. Giving up our rights is scary! It makes sense only if God is trustworthy.

PRAYER AND PRAISE REPORT

Briefly share your prayer requests with the large group, making notations below. Then gather in smaller groups of two to four to pray for each other.

Date: _____

Prayer Requests

_____

_____

_____

_____

_____

_____

_____

_____

_____

Praise Report

_____

_____

_____

_____

_____

_____

_____

_____

_____

_____

REFLECTIONS

Use this page to write out your prayers, your thoughts about your daily Bible reading, or your meditations on a verse from the passage you have already studied. Below are some suggested verses for meditation. The Bible Reading Plan is on pages 87–88.

For Meditation: Matthew 13:44 or Luke 9:25

For Gospel Reading:

- What do I *learn* from the life of Christ (his identity, personality, priorities)?

- How does he want me to *live* differently?

DVD NOTES

If you are watching the accompanying *Growing in Christ Together* DVD, write down what you sense God is saying to you through the speaker. (If you'd like to hear a sample of the DVD teaching segment, go to www.lifetogether.com/ExperiencingChristTogether.)

_____

_____

_____

_____

_____

_____

_____

_____

_____

_____

_____

_____

_____

_____

_____

_____

_____

_____

_____

_____

_____

_____

_____

THE POWER
OF THE DESERT

Bruce was a highly paid real estate executive. He never thought he would be let go. He was too important to the organization. But with slowdowns in commercial construction in the late 1980s, his company needed to downsize.

During several months of unemployment, Bruce thought about what God wanted him to do with his life. He resisted the temptation to jump quickly into another job—even though opportunities were readily available—and chose instead to take six months to seek God's direction. His friends thought that was too long. Bruce spent a lot of time alone—journaling, reading his Bible, and praying. He counseled with close friends, but mainly he listened to the Lord. Ultimately, Bruce felt God leading him not to return to real estate but to join the staff of a church as its men's ministry pastor. Bruce had been investing in men's lives as a businessman, and now he could pursue his passion full-time.

Unemployment can be a desert time: empty, dry, and scary. But Bruce used it as a chance to listen to God and grow in his faith and fruitfulness.

CONNECTING WITH GOD'S FAMILY   10 min.

1. In a typical week, how much time do you spend alone—not doing a task, being entertained, or sleeping? (This alone time could include time spent praying, thinking, relaxing in silence, or taking a quiet walk, for example.)

GROWING TO BE LIKE CHRIST   30–40 min.

Our culture tempts us to be full. We're supposed to be "consumers"—encouraged to consume entertainment, information, products, food, drink, exercise, and relationships until our hunger for stimulation is temporarily satisfied. We're also supposed to produce work, beautiful homes, perfect children, and even ministry until our world is full of the things we've accomplished. The more

stimulation, the better: play music while you work; edit the movie so that images flash faster and faster. We love it.

But before Jesus began his ministry, the Holy Spirit drove him into the desert for a time of emptiness. This wasn't an entertaining vacation at a desert resort with golf courses and flowing fountains. It was hot, dry, and lonely. In the same way, God sometimes empties and dries us out so he can fill us with his life. During times of emptiness, we become most dependent on God.

2. Read Luke 4:1–13. What did Jesus do during more than a month in the desert?

3. Read the study note for "if you are the Son of God." How did Satan challenge something important to Jesus in each of the three temptations?

4. How did these temptations cause Jesus to think more deeply about his mission?

5. God deliberately led Jesus into this time of emptiness and temptation. How did God use this hard experience for good?

6. Why do you suppose Jesus chose to fast?

7. In a desert time, all we have is ourselves and it's not enough. Have you ever had a desert time? If so, what do you think was the Devil's desire in that situation?

What was God's desire for you in that time?

8. The Devil wants to tempt you at your most vulnerable point. What might that be?

9. The Word of God helped Jesus keep reality in perspective while he struggled with temptation in the desert. Why do you suppose Jesus turned to the Scriptures to deal with temptation rather than handling it some other way?

10. What has helped you in times of temptation or dryness in the desert?

11. Jesus didn't own a Bible. Because Bibles were copied by hand in his day, they were fabulously expensive, as well as large. So the only way he could take God's Word to the desert was by committing lengthy portions of it to memory. Today the easy

accessibility of Bibles makes many of us take God's Word for granted. And memorizing seems impossible—after all, we have so much information thrown at us every day at work and through the media that our brains feel more than full.

Still, if you've never spent enough time in a Bible passage that it became part of you and sprang to your mind in the moment of need, then we urge you to try it. Look for the meditation verses on the Reflections page. Why not try just one verse for the next seven days?

FOR DEEPER STUDY

Read the context of the Old Testament passages Jesus quoted when he was tempted: Deuteronomy 6:4–19; 8:1–5, 17–18. Why do you think these were especially important passages for Jesus to learn by heart? How are these passages relevant to temptations you face?

The Israelites hated wandering in the desert; they wanted to get to the Promised Land. However, later God pointed out what the desert experience achieved (Deuteronomy 2:7; Jeremiah 2:2–3). What did it achieve? What have your desert times achieved?

How does Paul advise you to deal with the Devil's schemes (Ephesians 6:10–18)?

DEVELOPING YOUR GIFTS TO SERVE OTHERS   15 min.

One way you can serve someone else in your group is to team up to support each other in your spiritual growth. It's so much easier to keep going with a habit like prayer or Scripture meditation if you have a friend to cheer you on. If you've done another study in this series, you may already have a spiritual partner. If not, this is your chance to test drive a partnership! You won't believe how the Holy Spirit can work through this person.

12. Pair up with someone in your group. (We suggest that men partner with men and women with women.) This person will be your "spiritual partner" for the rest of this study. He or she doesn't have to be your best friend but will simply encourage you to complete the goal you set for your spiritual growth in session 1. If you already have a spiritual partner from another study in this series, you may keep the same partner or switch to a new one.

13. On pages 34–35 is a tracking chart entitled Personal Health Plan. In the box that says, "WHO are you connecting with spiritually?" write your partner's name. In the box that says, "WHAT is your next step for growth?" write the step you chose in question 11 of session 1.

    Tell your partner what step you chose. When you check in with your partner each week, this chart will remind you of your partner's step and will provide a place to record his or her progress as well as your own. On pages 84–85 you'll find a completed health plan filled in as an example. Also, if you have more than one partner, another copy of the health plan is on pages 82–83.

SURRENDERING YOUR LIFE FOR GOD'S PLEASURE   15 min.

14. Are you going through a desert experience now—a time when you feel dry or empty or sense an area where you are vulnerable to temptation? If so, tell your group.

    Gather around anyone who is experiencing a desert and pray for this person. If you feel comfortable doing so, lay a hand on the person's shoulder.

15. A great way to close this session is to play one of the slower songs from the DVD or the LIFE TOGETHER Worship series. Play it once without singing, while everyone listens with eyes closed. Then play it again and quietly sing to the Father as a prayer.

STUDY NOTES

Forty days (Luke 4:2). The forty days Jesus spent in the desert echo the forty years the Israelites were forced to wander in the desert after God freed them from slavery in Egypt. Israel's desert time tested the people's faith and obedience, just as Jesus' desert time did. It was a time to be stripped of self-dependence. Israel frequently failed their tests; Jesus fulfilled what Israel failed to fulfill.

Jesus' long solitude wasn't just a test; it was also preparation for the stressful ministry he was about to begin. Without even food, he was empty of everything but the Holy Spirit (Luke 4:1). Desert times teach us to crave what only God can give us: himself.

If you are the Son of God (4:3, 9). Satan targeted Jesus' most important and most vulnerable point: his identity. How would the Son of God live out his sonship? Could he be tempted to use power over people and the natural world to feed selfish appetites for food, control, fame, invulnerability? Could he be lured away from using his power in service to God and others? Could his calling be twisted with self-importance so that every act would be subtly self-serving? The Devil didn't know Jesus' mission was to die on our behalf, but he knew that Jesus had something crucial to do, and that the way to thwart it was to twist it.

It is written . . . It says (4:4, 8, 12). Three times the Devil tempted Jesus, and three times Jesus quoted chapters 6–8 of the Old Testament book of Deuteronomy. Deuteronomy contains the parting words of Israel's greatest prophet, Moses, at the end of Israel's forty-year exile in the desert. The nation was about to begin the mission God had planned for them. Moses told them the truths about God and themselves they must take to heart in order to do this. Because Jesus' job was to fulfill what Israel failed to fulfill, it made sense that he memorized these words.

Jesus used God's Word to defend himself against Satan's schemes (Ephesians 6:11). Responding with the truth sets us free (John 8:32).

He left him until an opportune time (4:13). Satan doesn't let us rest. He keeps seeking us like a "roaring lion" (1 Peter 5:8). Even after God leads us out of a time of emptiness, Satan will continue to stalk us. He'll tempt us to think we got through the hard time on our own (pride). He will try to get us to use our gifts to serve ourselves. We need to be on guard at all times, fully dependent on God.

PRAYER AND PRAISE REPORT

Briefly share your prayer requests with the large group, making notations below. Then gather in smaller groups of two to four to pray for each other.

Date: _____

Prayer Requests

_____

_____

_____

_____

_____

_____

_____

_____

_____

_____

Praise Report

_____

_____

_____

_____

_____

_____

_____

_____

_____

_____

_____

REFLECTIONS

Use this page to write out your prayers, your thoughts about your daily Bible reading, or your meditations on a verse from the passage you have already studied. Below are some suggested verses for meditation. The Bible Reading Plan is on pages 87–88.

For Meditation: Luke 4:8, Luke 4:12, or Matthew 4:4

For Gospel Reading:

- What do I *learn* from the life of Christ (his identity, personality, priorities)?

- How does he want me to *live* differently?

DVD NOTES

If you are watching the accompanying *Growing in Christ Together* DVD, write down what you sense God saying to you through the speaker. (If you'd like to hear a sample of the DVD teaching segment, go to www.lifeto-gether.com/ExperiencingChristTogether.)

_____

_____

_____

_____

_____

_____

_____

_____

_____

_____

_____

_____

_____

_____

_____

_____

_____

_____

_____

_____

_____

_____

_____

_____

_____

_____

_____

PERSONAL HEALTH PLAN

This worksheet could become your single most important feature in this study. On it you can record your personal priorities before the Father. It will help you live a healthy spiritual life, balancing all five of God's purposes.

PURPOSE	PLAN
CONNECT	WHO are you connecting with spiritually?
GROW	WHAT is your next step for growth?
DEVELOP	WHERE are you serving?
SHARE	WHEN are you shepherding another in Christ?
SURRENDER	HOW are you surrendering your heart?

If you have more than one partner, another Personal Health Plan can be found in the Appendix or downloaded in a larger format at www.lifetogether.com/healthplan. A Sample Health Plan is also in the Appendix.

DATE	MY PROGRESS	PARTNER'S PROGRESS

PRESSING THE PAUSE BUTTON

Little things used to make Justin lose his temper with his wife, kids, and coworkers. He got frustrated with other drivers on the road. In fact, frustration simmered inside him all the time. He prayed about it, but his temper problem wouldn't go away.

Then a friend helped him recognize a key factor in his frustration. He set high standards for how much he had to get done in a given day. He needed to get ahead in his job, so he needed to be highly productive. So he needed to work longer hours. So he needed to fit in his errands after work more efficiently. So he needed to drive from point A to point B as fast as possible. But the world wouldn't cooperate with his demand that it hurry up.

With divine help, Justin gradually lowered his expectations of himself. He forced himself to plan several hours a week alone with God. Those hours that felt so "unproductive" became vastly productive in shaping his character. As Justin came to terms with his own limits, he grew more tolerant of others' limits too. He had to choose between moving slower and loving people better *or* getting more done but hurting more people. He chose the slow lane.

For some of us, taking time out is the biggest thing we can do for our spiritual growth. In this session you'll look at the rhythm of Jesus' life to see how it compares to your own.

CONNECTING WITH GOD'S FAMILY   10 min.

You can begin this session in one of two ways. You can let spiritual partners check in to support one another's growth (question 2), or you can start everyone thinking about this session's theme by taking a quick self-assessment.

1. For each of the following questions, raise your hand if your answer is yes.

    ☐ Do you often drive more than five miles over the speed limit?

☐ When you stand in line at a store, do you watch the other lines to see if they are moving faster than yours?

☐ Do you often do two things at once (such as checking email while eating lunch, or talking on the phone while driving)?

☐ Do you skip meals so you can get more work done?

☐ Do you feel rushed?

Or,

2. Sit with your spiritual partner(s). If your partner is absent, join with another pair or with someone whose partner is also absent. How has your personal time with God (prayer, Bible reading, meditation, or journaling) been going? What have you learned? If you've had trouble getting time alone with God, what obstacles have hindered you?

GROWING TO BE LIKE CHRIST   30–40 min.

Hurry is a disease in our culture. Your world isn't just telling you to produce more, more, more. It's telling you to do it faster, faster, faster.

Hurrying interferes with your number-one life priority: love. Jesus said God's top two instructions for life are to love God with everything you've got and to love your neighbors as you love yourself (Matthew 22:34–40). But "faster, faster, faster" makes you annoyed with the person driving the car ahead of you, impatient with your toddler who takes forever to get dressed, overwhelmed with all you're expected to accomplish at work, and frustrated with yourself for failing to meet your world's demands. It also makes you too busy to spend relaxed, attentive, enjoyable time with God. It's hard to love when you're annoyed, overwhelmed, or unavailable. And it's hard to hear from God.

Jesus faced similar pressures. Once word got around that he could heal the sick, he was besieged by people in need. How did he respond?

3. Read the following passages. In each case, describe what was going on when Jesus decided to go off by himself to pray.
Mark 1:32–39

Luke 5:15–16

Mark 6:30–46

4. From these passages, what do you think motivated Jesus to seek times of solitude?

5. What pressures to give up these solitary times did he face?

6. How do you think other people benefited from the time Jesus spent in solitary prayer?

7. What relationship do you see between public ministry and solitary prayer in Jesus' life?

8. When you take a break from work and/or ministry, what do you typically do with your time?

9. How might other people benefit from time you spend (or could spend) in solitude and prayer?

10. What motivates you to spend time in solitude and prayer?

11. What hinders you from doing so?

12. If we want to leave a wide door open for God to use us, we need to keep a small backdoor open to rid ourselves of things that we need to let go. What can you let go of to make time for solitude and prayer?

FOR DEEPER STUDY

How did Jesus handle pressure from his family to speed up his ministry and build his fame (John 7:1–10, 14)?

How did Jesus deal with a situation in which a child needed urgent attention but another sick person needed attention too (Mark 5:21–43)?

What do these scenes tell you about Jesus' ability to listen to his Father? What do they tell you about his attitude toward people and relationships? How is Jesus' example relevant to situations you face?

DEVELOPING YOUR GIFTS TO SERVE OTHERS   15–20 min.

13. We strongly suggest that you go on a half-day or full-day retreat as a group. Ideas for planning such a retreat are on pages 94–96. Who in your group would be interested if a good time and place can be found? Which two group members would be willing to take charge of scheduling and planning the retreat?

14. Is your response to a retreat something like this: "There's no way I can take a day off from my busy life anytime in the next six months. When I'm not working, I'm shuttling kids around or doing things for my church or fixing things around the house or ..."? If so, what would it take for you to make this kind of space in your life for God? Have an honest discussion about the obstacles you face.

SURRENDERING YOUR LIFE FOR GOD'S PLEASURE   15–30 min.

15. Take a moment of quiet to write on the Reflections page in this session. Finish the sentence: "Father, I need Your help today with ..."

    If time allows and you are willing, share what you wrote with your partner, a friend, or your spouse. The Bible urges us to carry each other's burdens (Galatians 6:2). Take a risk!

STUDY NOTES

Jesus knew his disciples were watching how he carried himself in ministry and relationships. He modeled for them a rhythm of active ministry and time alone with the Father.

The whole town gathered at the door (Mark 1:33). Capernaum was one of many villages scattered around the Sea of Galilee. Travelers from various countries probably passed through the town, buying and selling before heading south toward Egypt and beyond. Jesus made Capernaum his home because his friend Peter lived there. Jews and Gentiles would have gathered to see Jesus perform miracles and hear him teach in the synagogue just a few hundred feet from Peter's house. With no real medical care available, a rabbi with healing powers would have attracted hundreds of sick and disabled persons.

The apostles ... reported to him (6:30). After Jesus' twelve core disciples had watched him teach and heal for many months, he named them "apostles" (Greek: sent ones) and sent them out in pairs to do what they had seen him do. We don't know how long they were on the road, but when they returned, they reported what had happened.

Did not even have a chance to eat (6:31). By this time, Jesus was a celebrity thronged by people. Some were desperate for healing, while others hoped he was the messiah-king who would lead a rebellion against Rome (John 6:14–15).

They went away by themselves (6:32). It's not clear from the passage whether the apostles got some time to rest before the crowd found them and Jesus responded with compassion (6:34). Mark often used a "sandwich" technique in his writing style. In this case, he sandwiched the story of Jesus' active compassion toward the crowd between two scenes where Jesus sought rest and solitude for the apostles (6:31–32) and for himself (6:45–46).

PRAYER AND PRAISE REPORT

Briefly share your prayer requests with the large group, making notations below. Then gather in smaller groups of two to four to pray for each other.

Date: _____

Prayer Requests

_____

_____

_____

_____

_____

_____

_____

_____

_____

_____

Praise Report

_____

_____

_____

_____

_____

_____

_____

_____

_____

_____

_____

REFLECTIONS

Use this page to write out your prayers, your thoughts about your daily Bible reading, or your meditations on a verse from the passage you have already studied. Below are some suggested verses for meditation. The Bible Reading Plan is on pages 87–88.

For Meditation: Mark 1:36–38 or 6:31

For Gospel Reading:

- What do I *learn* from the life of Christ (his identity, personality, priorities)?

- How does he want me to *live* differently?

_____

_____

_____

_____

_____

_____

_____

_____

_____

_____

_____

_____

_____

_____

_____

_____

_____

_____

_____

DVD NOTES

If you are watching the accompanying *Growing in Christ Together* DVD, write down what you sense God saying to you through the speaker. (If you'd like to hear a sample of the DVD teaching segment, go to www.lifetogether.com/ExperiencingChristTogether.)

_____

_____

_____

_____

_____

_____

_____

_____

_____

_____

_____

_____

_____

_____

_____

_____

_____

_____

_____

_____

_____

4 PERSISTENT PRAYER

From the age of eight, Denise prayed that her dad would accept Christ and spend eternity in heaven. She prayed with small groups. She prayed alone, begging God to answer. She asked large groups to pray. She prayed at camp. She questioned God's plan and wondered if God really desired *all* people to know him. After all, she adored her father, and why wouldn't God bring her father to Christ?

After thirty-two years, her dad, Densil, still did not want to know Christ. In recent years, Denise prayed that God would use whatever it would take. She prayed that he would use her life or someone else's for her dad to see Christ. Last July, God used colon cancer. At the age of sixty-two, Densil was diagnosed with terminal cancer. Denise would never wish cancer for anyone—the pain, the sadness, the brutality—but now Densil has committed his life to Christ. Now she and her dad experience the fellowship of the Lord and the sweetness of knowing him together. Now they will spend eternity together, seeing the Lord face to face. God answered her persistent prayer, not in a time or a way of her choosing, but faithfully nonetheless.

CONNECTING WITH GOD'S FAMILY   20 min.

Again, you may choose either the question for the whole group (question 1) or the chance for spiritual partners to connect (question 2).

1. When you were a child, what typically happened when you asked your parents for help?

   Or,

2. Sit with your spiritual partner. If your partner is absent, join another pair or someone else who is missing a partner. What happened in your personal time with God this week? Share something from your journal.

GROWING TO BE LIKE CHRIST

When Jesus taught his disciples to pray, he focused on their picture of God. If we pray as though God is mean, busy, or distracted, then we aren't talking to the real God. If we pray as though we call the shots and it's God's job to do what we want, again we aren't talking to the real God. Jesus wanted his disciples to pray from hearts of love to a Father who loved them.

3. Read Luke 11:1–13. Jesus begins his lesson with a sample prayer (verses 2–4). What picture of God do you get from this prayer? What must God be like if we're supposed to address him like this and ask for these things?

4. Next, Jesus tells a story (verses 5–8). What motivates the man to get out of bed at midnight to give bread to his neighbor?

5. Jesus tells quirky stories like the one in verses 5–8 to help us think. Is God like a guy who goes to bed and says, "Don't bother me"? What do you suppose Jesus wants us to get out of this story?

6. Jesus says the man's "boldness" (verse 8) gets results even with a sleepy friend. How bold are you in prayer? Why do you suppose that's the case?

7. Jesus gets to the bottom line in verses 9–13. What picture of God does he paint in these verses?

8. Perhaps you feel like you've asked God for an egg and he's given you a scorpion. Or maybe you grew up in the kind of family where asking for even an egg was risky. Share with the group any past experiences that make it hard for you to trust that God the Father is the way Jesus presents him.

9. Pause to pray for anyone in the group who has shared something difficult in question 8. Ask God to send his Holy Spirit to heal the scar from this memory and give this person a true picture of the Father.

10. Jesus encourages us to ask, seek, and knock boldly—for the Holy Spirit's active presence in our lives (verse 13). Why for the Holy Spirit, and not for the million other things we might want?

11. Your homework assignment for this week is to spend half an hour alone with God. During this time, you can't do Bible study or read a book. Tell God whatever is on your mind, or just sit with him. Take a walk with him. If your mind wanders, you might write him a letter in your journal. Everybody's mind wanders, so there's no need to stress over it. Take your whole self, wandering mind and all, to the Father who loves you as passionately as he ever loved anybody.

FOR DEEPER STUDY

Read Matthew's account of Jesus' teaching on prayer in Matthew 6:5–15. What additional insights do you find?

What attitudes about God and life does Paul urge us to keep at the front of our minds in Philippians 4:4–7? Which of these are easy for you, and which are not?

In 1 Thessalonians 5:17, Paul exhorts us to "pray continually." How do you think a person goes about doing that in a practical way?

In Romans 8:5–8 and Colossians 3:2–3, Paul emphasizes the importance of what we set our minds on—what we let ourselves habitually think about. What should we routinely do with our minds? What shouldn't we do? How do Paul's words here help you understand the purpose of constant, intimate prayer?

DEVELOPING YOUR GIFTS TO SERVE OTHERS   15–20 min.

12. Give the people in charge of planning your retreat a few minutes to update the group on their progress.

13. Every member of your group, not just the leader, is a minister in the body of Christ. God wants you to discover how he has uniquely designed you to serve him and to develop your gifts over time. You'll discover and develop your gifts as you experiment with different ways to serve and practice service consistently.

   In a previous LIFE TOGETHER study you may have tried an area of service, such as hosting a social event. We encourage you to take the next step by teaming up with someone else in your group to champion one of the five purposes of the church.

Assuming your group plans to continue meeting after the end of this study, which purpose are you willing to help with for the next six weeks? Instructions for creating teams for each purpose are on pages 77–79.

 SURRENDERING YOUR LIFE FOR GOD'S PLEASURE 15–30 min.

14. Jesus urges us to be bold and persistent in our prayers. Turn to your Prayer and Praise Report on page 51. What one request on this list are you willing to pray about persistently for the next three weeks?

15. Gather into smaller circles of three or four people. Have an extended time of prayer. Start by telling God honestly how you see him. Do you see him as your tender Father, or as something else? Then ask him for what you need: bread, forgiveness, his Holy Spirit.

STUDY NOTES

Father (Luke 11:2). Jesus gives us permission to talk to the Creator of the universe in an astonishingly intimate, approachable way. This is extremely rare in the history of world religions. The all-powerful God regards us as family.

Hallowed (11:2). To hallow something is to treat it as holy, sacred, worthy of awe and respect. For Jews, God's name represented his identity and character. We are intimate family with Someone who deserves awe, Someone whose character is so excellent that he deserves to be respected and even imitated.

Kingdom (11:2). Recall the definition of the kingdom from session 1.

Don't bother me (11:7). Middle Eastern culture was built on honor and shame. Hospitality was a matter of honor, so the host with a visiting friend absolutely *had* to get food for him. The honor of the host, his family, and the whole village was at stake. The neighbor's boldness (verse 8) was motivated by desperate need.

Likewise, a neighbor who asked for help almost always received a positive response. To say no was to shame both the one who asked and the whole community. Jesus' listeners knew this and would have been shocked at the man who told his neighbor to go away. Jesus was saying, "If even this unbelievably rude person eventually responded to bold and persistent requests, how do you think God behaves?"

Egg ... scorpion (11:12). We don't receive just because we ask; we receive because God's nature is compassionate, loving, and caring. God isn't angry or stingy. He wants to help us and minimize our pain. He allows painful situations as part of his larger plan for our good and the good of the whole world, but he isn't pleased to make us suffer. Some of us have been hurt and disappointed, and wonder why God doesn't seem to be doing anything about it. We need to be persistent, trusting that God cares and will provide what we need (Philippians 4:19). Even when God allows us to suffer tragedy and there's no obvious reason why, we need to trust that in the big picture of his plan for us and those we love, he will bring good even out of evil.

PRAYER AND PRAISE REPORT

Briefly share your prayer requests with the large group, making notations below. Then gather in smaller groups of two to four to pray for each other.

Date: _____

Prayer Requests

_____

_____

_____

_____

_____

_____

_____

_____

_____

Praise Report

_____

_____

_____

_____

_____

_____

_____

_____

_____

_____

REFLECTIONS

Use this page to write out your prayers, your thoughts about your daily Bible reading, or your meditations on a verse from the passage you have already studied. Below are some suggested verses for meditation. The Bible Reading Plan is on pages 87–88.

For Meditation: Luke 11:2–4, 11:9, or 11:13

For Gospel Reading:

- What do I *learn* from the life of Christ (his identity, personality, priorities)?

- How does he want me to *live* differently?

DVD NOTES

If you are watching the accompanying *Growing in Christ Together* DVD, write down what you sense God saying to you through the speaker. (If you'd like to hear a sample of the DVD teaching segment, go to www.lifeto-gether.com/ExperiencingChristTogether.)

SESSION 5

BUILDING ON A SOLID FOUNDATION

Some years ago, Dave went looking to buy his first house. After several months, he finally found one that had all the appearances of being "the one." It was cute with a tiny yard, a white picket fence, and within walking distance to the beach. His family gave him the thumbs-up. He couldn't go wrong, they thought. But when Dave had the house inspected, he learned it had a huge crack in the foundation. Even so, it was painful for Dave to let it go. He had already decorated it in his mind. But with a poor foundation, the house wasn't worth much, especially in California! The slightest earthquake could crack this house in two.

Foundations aren't seen, but they're essential to a sturdy home. Many believers try to live life without a firm foundation. They look great until one of life's inevitable storms or quakes hits them. All too often, their faith crumbles into panic or bitterness at God. Nothing makes Christ sadder.

CONNECTING WITH GOD'S FAMILY   10 min.

Allow time either for the whole group to check in with each other (question 1) or for spiritual partners to connect (question 2).

1. How's the weather in your life right now?

   ☐ Warm and sunny
   ☐ Partly cloudy with a chance of showers
   ☐ A slow, steady drizzle
   ☐ Pouring rain with flood warnings
   ☐ Hurricane!

   Or,

2. Sit with your spiritual partner. What has been happening in your personal time with the Lord?

GROWING TO BE LIKE CHRIST   30–40 min.

Solitude, slowing down, and deep prayer are all essential if we want to grow more like Christ. Doing less, or even nothing for a period of time, can be extremely fruitful for our souls. But at some point, we have to do something! We need to be like Christ in his quiet moments *and* in his active obedience to his Father.

Deep obedience results from a heart healed by God's love. Until we trust God to love and heal us, either we will obey him as a dictator (who seems to make demands on us for his own ends), or we will disobey him. We'll view his instructions as irrational or impossible, as threats to our deepest needs. "You want me to love my enemies? You're insane!" But for Jesus, deep obedience came naturally because he knew his Father's love.

3. For many people today, "obedience" evokes negative images and feelings. Why do you suppose that's the case?

4. Read Luke 6:46–49. How might a typical Christian answer the question Jesus poses in verse 46?

5. In verses 47–49, Jesus contrasts two kinds of people. What's the key difference between the foundations on which they build their lives?

6. When the storms of life hit us, many of us think God isn't doing his job. What do you learn about life's storms from this passage?

7. Luke 6:46–49 comes at the end of a chapter in which Jesus gives extensive instruction on how to lay a solid foundation for life. There's more than enough in just Luke 6:27–45 to start obeying! Read Luke 6:27–45. What instructions does Jesus give for a solid foundation?

8. Many people would say that to "do good to those who hate you" (Luke 6:27) is impractical and foolish. Yet Jesus says that to ignore this command, or others in this passage, is to build your house with a flawed foundation. Why would obeying this command help you withstand life's storms?

9. Jesus says the wise person puts his words into practice habitually, *before* a storm hits. Why do you suppose it's important to make a habit of obedience in the calm times?

10. As we said previously, unless we trust God to have our best interests at heart, we will obey him fearfully, if at all. How would knowing that God is committed to your good help you obey an instruction like "do good to those who hate you"?

FOR DEEPER STUDY

Read Matthew's version of this session's passage (Matthew 7:24–27). What does Matthew emphasize that Luke doesn't?

Study Jesus' commands in Luke 6:20–45. Why is each of these important as a foundation for life?

Read James 2:14–26. How does obedience demonstrate the quality of our faith?

DEVELOPING YOUR GIFTS TO SERVE OTHERS　　15 min.

11. Give the people who are planning your retreat a few minutes to update the group on their progress.

SURRENDERING YOUR LIFE FOR GOD'S PLEASURE　15–30 min.

12. What is one area where you think Jesus is asking for obedience from you? How can the group pray for you in this?

13. Some in your group may be facing a storm in their lives right now. If so, pray especially for those people. Gathering around them and placing a hand on their shoulder while you pray is a great way to express your care. If you are one of those who are in a hard place, please don't be embarrassed to ask the group to pray for you. People will consider it a privilege.

STUDY NOTES

Jesus modeled obedience to the Father. In John 17:4 he said, "I have brought you glory on earth by completing the work you gave me to do." His disciples knew that obedience was essential to discipleship. A disciple is not just a learner but a follower. He obediently follows Jesus and his wishes.

Hears . . . puts them into practice (Luke 6:47). The contrast isn't between hearing and not hearing. It's between doing and not doing. We can hear excellent Bible-based preaching and have no better foundation than someone who never goes to church. Obedience is paramount to a firm foundation. If we fail to act on what we believe, then we actually believe nothing and will eventually be all washed up.

Flood (6:48). Rain is seasonal in Palestine. Many areas are desert dry for most of the year but flood during the rainy seasons. Life is like that sometimes: we coast along during the sunny times, but when the rain starts, it's a deluge.

Nobody gets through life without hitting storms. Some storms are worse than others, and devotion to Christ is no guarantee that you won't suffer a hurricane. But consistently *hearing* and *practicing* Jesus' words will help you survive the experience and even have something to offer others.

PRAYER AND PRAISE REPORT

Briefly share your prayer requests with the large group, making notations below. Then gather in smaller groups of two to four to pray for each other.

Date: _____

Prayer Requests

_____

_____

_____

_____

_____

_____

_____

_____

_____

_____

Praise Report

_____

_____

_____

_____

_____

_____

_____

_____

_____

_____

_____

REFLECTIONS

Use this page to write out your prayers, your thoughts about your daily Bible reading, or your meditations on a verse from the passage you have already studied. Below are some suggested verses for meditation. The Bible Reading Plan is on pages 87–88.

For Meditation: Luke 6:46 or 6:47–49

For Gospel Reading:

- What do I *learn* from the life of Christ (his identity, personality, priorities)?

- How does he want me to *live* differently?

_____

_____

_____

_____

_____

_____

_____

_____

_____

_____

_____

_____

_____

_____

_____

_____

_____

_____

_____

_____

DVD NOTES

If you are watching the accompanying *Growing in Christ Together* DVD, write down what you sense God saying to you through the speaker. (If you'd like to hear a sample of the DVD teaching segment, go to www.lifetogether.com/ExperiencingChristTogether.)

_____

_____

_____

_____

_____

_____

_____

_____

_____

_____

_____

_____

_____

_____

_____

_____

_____

_____

_____

_____

_____

_____

_____

_____

WHERE'S YOUR TREASURE?

A financial planner urged thirty-year-old Sharon to plan her budget with the future in mind. She needed to start saving for retirement then, not put it off until her fifties. So Sharon began putting a little money each month into several stock mutual funds. The stock market boomed, and by the time Sharon was forty, her financial future was looking rosy.

Then the dot.com bubble burst. In eighteen months, half of Sharon's stock portfolio evaporated. She felt cheated. She had been wise and frugal. She hadn't spent her paychecks accumulating "stuff" the way her friend Hannah did. Hannah still had her stuff, but Sharon didn't.

Eventually, Sharon realized that although she had been saving rather than spending, her attitude toward money was much like Hannah's. Hannah relied on money to make her life feel good; Sharon relied on money to make her life feel safe. Both women relied on money for what felt most important.

Sharon has learned that money is a useful tool but an unreliable master. She's back to saving for retirement—cautiously—but she knows that her true safety is in eternal life with God.

And Hannah? She had to rent a storage unit to store things that wouldn't fit in her apartment. After spending a thousand dollars on storing things she never used, she found out that there are about "31,000 self-storage facilities in the United States . . . with each . . . averaging 55,000 square feet."[1] Hannah decided she didn't want to contribute to almost two billion square feet of hoarded possessions. She gave a lot of hers away.

Whether we're packrats, big spenders, or living lean, we all need to think about what we treasure and why.

---

[1]Victoria Clayton, "Psychology by the Square Foot," *Los Angeles Times Magazine* (August 10, 2003), 12.

CONNECTING WITH GOD'S FAMILY   10 min.

Choose either the question for the whole group (question 1) or the one for spiritual partners (question 2).

1. Which of these statements best describes the way you handle money?

   ☐ I am frugal and like to save money.
   ☐ I have trouble saving money and tend to spend it on possessions.
   ☐ I have trouble saving money and tend to spend it on experiences.
   ☐ I have trouble saving money and tend to spend it on other people.
   ☐ None of the above. (Please explain.)

   Or,

2. Check in with your spiritual partner. What has God been teaching you? How can your partner encourage you? Share something from your journal.

GROWING TO BE LIKE CHRIST   30–40 min.

In session 1 you discussed a man who sold everything to buy a treasure. This session comes back to that idea of treasure. For Jesus, your treasure or your master is whatever you focus on, whatever you value most highly. If you're having trouble overcoming busyness, for example, the problem may be too many competing priorities. You may need to narrow your focus to what's most important.

Jesus taught his disciples to value "the kingdom of heaven," that is, the realm where God dwells, the eternal life that starts now. If you yearn to experience that life, you'll need to make cuts in other areas.

3. Read Matthew 6:19–24. Here Jesus talks about something many people focus on: money. What reasons does he give for not treasuring, serving, or focusing on money?

4. Have you experienced the truth of any of these reasons? If so, please explain.

5. Read Matthew 6:25–34. Jesus says the clue to whether we're focusing too much on money or other desires is worry (verse 25). What do you tend to worry about?

6. What are some of the desires behind your worries?

I want/need _____.

7. In verses 25–34, what reasons does Jesus give for not worrying about the things we desire?

8. It boils down to how we see God. For some of us, it's hard to truly believe that our heavenly Father knows what we need (verse 32) and will provide it. What are some of the reasons why we doubt this?

9. What do you think it means to "seek first his kingdom and his righteousness" (verse 33)?

10. How can you seek God's kingdom over the next month or so? What will you need to focus on less?

FOR DEEPER STUDY

Paul said that what you build your life with will either be destroyed or last forever (1 Corinthians 3:10–15). What life priorities count as gold, silver, and precious stones that will last into eternity? What life priorities count as wood, hay, and straw that leave a person with nothing after death except his or her bare salvation?

In Luke 18:18–23, Jesus tells a rich man how to get treasure in heaven. What does this man need to do? Why is that an important step for him? How do you think Jesus' instruction to this man is relevant to you?

What further teaching on money do you find in 1 Timothy 6:17–19? How are Paul's words relevant to you?

SHARING YOUR LIFE MISSION EVERY DAY   15–20 min.

11. Give the people in charge of planning your retreat a few minutes to confirm their final plans with the group.

12. How has this group helped you grow spiritually? What are you thankful for?

13. What's next for your group? This study has emphasized the "do less" disciplines (solitude, silence, slowness, prayer) that can help you become the person God made you to be. By doing less in these areas, you will have space in your life to seek God's kingdom. Three active ways you can seek God's kingdom are service, outreach, and celebration. The study in this series called *Serving Like Christ Together* focuses on serving others. *Sharing Christ Together* deals with reaching out to unbelievers. *Surrendering to Christ Together* addresses celebrating God. These active habits are as important as the quiet ones for healthy, balanced spiritual growth.

14. Turn to the LIFE TOGETHER Agreement on pages 74–75. Is there anything you'd like the group to do better as it moves forward?

SURRENDERING YOUR LIFE FOR GOD'S PLEASURE   15–30 min.

15. How did you do with the goal you set for yourself in your Personal Health Plan (pages 34–35)? Let the whole group know so they can celebrate with you.

16. Turn to your Prayer and Praise Report and let members update the group on any answered prayers. Then have a time of worship to thank God for what he's been doing in your lives. Use some songs from the DVD, the LIFE TOGETHER DVD/CD Worship series, or a CD of your choice. Or read one or two psalms together, such as Psalm 66, 77, or 84. You could have half the group read the even-numbered verses and the other half read the odd-numbered ones.

STUDY NOTES

Treasures (Matthew 6:19). A treasure is anything you value highly. Jesus' words about storing up treasures on earth are forceful: "Don't do it." It will only wreak havoc in your life. It will distract you from things that last into eternity, such as loving people and serving God. Jesus doesn't condemn careful planning for the future. He condemns hoarding wealth or things. Each of us needs to decide where the line between prudent saving and ungodly hoarding should be drawn.

The lamp of the body (6:22). In ancient Israel, a lamp was extremely important. It was the only source of light at night, other than the moon. There were no streetlights, and homes had only one or two lamps. So whatever a lamp illumined was what people focused their attention on. The eye is the body's lamp. Whatever the eye focuses on is what the person focuses on. If the eye focuses on what is eternal, it brings light (truth, eternity) into the person. If the eye focuses on what is temporary, such as possessions, money, or status, it brings darkness (delusion or sin) to the person. What the eye focuses on either corrupts or purifies a person at the core. What are you focusing on?

Masters (6:24). Either money or God will own you. Which do you want to become a slave to? You can decide who or what you want to serve in this life and the life to come. D. A. Carson said, "Either God is served with a single-eyed devotion, or he is not served at all. Attempts at divided loyalty betray, not partial commitment to discipleship, but deep-seated commitment to idolatry."[2]

Kingdom (6:33). See the definition in session 1.

---

[2]D. A. Carson, "Matthew," *The Expositor's Bible Commentary, New Testament,* Frank E. Gaebelein, gen. ed., in Zondervan Reference Software, version 2.8 (Grand Rapids: Zondervan, 1998).

PRAYER AND PRAISE REPORT

Briefly share your prayer requests with the large group, making notations below. Then gather in smaller groups of two to four to pray for each other.

Date: _____

Prayer Requests

_____
_____
_____
_____
_____
_____
_____
_____
_____
_____

Praise Report

_____
_____
_____
_____
_____
_____
_____
_____
_____
_____
_____

REFLECTIONS

Use this page to write out your prayers, your thoughts about your daily Bible reading, or your meditations on a verse from the passage you have already studied. Below are some suggested verses for meditation. The Bible Reading Plan is on pages 87–88.

For Meditation: Matthew 6:21, 6:24, or 6:33

For Gospel Reading:

- What do I *learn* from the life of Christ (his identity, personality, priorities)?

- How does he want me to *live* differently?

DVD NOTES

If you are watching the accompanying *Growing in Christ Together* DVD, write down what you sense God saying to you through the speaker. (If you'd like to hear a sample of the DVD teaching segment, go to www.lifetogether.com/ExperiencingChristTogether.)

_____

_____

_____

_____

_____

_____

_____

_____

_____

_____

_____

_____

_____

_____

_____

_____

_____

_____

_____

_____

_____

_____

_____

FREQUENTLY ASKED QUESTIONS

What do we do on the first night of our group?

Like all fun things in life—have a party! A "get to know you" coffee, dinner, or dessert is a great way to launch a new study. You may want to review the LIFE TOGETHER Agreement (pages 74–75) and share the names of a few friends you can invite to join you. But most importantly, have fun before your study time begins.

Where do we find new members for our group?

This can be troubling, especially for new groups that have only a few people or for existing groups that lose a few people along the way. We encourage you to pray with your group and then brainstorm a list of people from work, church, your neighborhood, your children's school, family, the gym, and so forth. Then have each group member invite several of the people on his or her list. Another good strategy is to ask church leaders to make an announcement or allow a bulletin insert.

No matter how you find members, it's vital that you stay on the lookout for new people to join your group. All groups tend to go through healthy attrition—the result of moves, releasing new leaders, ministry opportunities, and so forth—and if the group gets too small, it could be at risk of shutting down. If you and your group stay open, you'll be amazed at the people God sends your way. The next person just might become a friend for life. You never know!

How long will this group meet?

It's totally up to the group—once you come to the end of this six-week study. Most groups meet weekly for at least the first six weeks, but every other week can work as well. We strongly recommend that the group meet for the first six months on a weekly basis if at all possible. This allows for continuity, and if people miss a meeting they aren't gone for a whole month.

At the end of this study, each group member may decide if he or she wants to continue on for another six-week study. Some groups launch relationships for years to come, and others are stepping-stones into another group experience. Either way, enjoy the journey.

Can we do this study on our own?

Absolutely! This may sound crazy but one of the best ways to do this study is not with a full house but with a few friends. You may choose to gather with one other couple who would enjoy going to the movies or having a quiet dinner and then walking through this study. Jesus will be with you even if there are only two of you (Matthew 18:20).

What if this group is not working for us?

You're not alone! This could be the result of a personality conflict, life stage difference, geographical distance, level of spiritual maturity, or any number of things. Relax. Pray for God's direction, and at the end of this six-week study, decide whether to continue with this group or find another. You don't buy the first car you look at or marry the first person you date, and the same goes with a group. Don't bail out before the six weeks are up—God might have something to teach you. Also, don't run from conflict or prejudge people before you have given them a chance. God is still working in you too!

Who is the leader?

Most groups have an official leader. But ideally, the group will mature and members will rotate the leadership of meetings. We have discovered that healthy groups rotate hosts/leaders and homes on a regular basis. This model ensures that all members grow, give their unique contribution, and develop their gifts. This study guide and the Holy Spirit can keep things on track even when you rotate leaders. Christ has promised to be in your midst as you gather. Ultimately, God is your leader each step of the way.

How do we handle the child care needs in our group?

Very carefully. Seriously, this can be a sensitive issue. We suggest that you empower the group to openly brainstorm solutions. You may try one option that works for a while and then adjust over time. Our favorite approach is for adults to meet in the living room or dining room, and to share the cost of a babysitter (or two) who can be with the kids in a different part of the house. In this way, parents don't have to be away from their children all evening when their children are too young to be left at home. A second option is to use one home for the kids and a second home (close by or a phone call away) for the adults. A third idea is to rotate the responsibility of providing a lesson or care for the children either in the same home or in another home nearby. This can be an incredible blessing for kids. Finally, the most common idea is to decide that you need to have a night to invest in your spiritual lives individually or as a couple, and to make your own arrangements for child care. No matter what decision the group makes, the best approach is to dialogue openly about both the problem and the solution.

To answer your further questions, we have created a website called www.lifetogether.com/ExperiencingChristTogether that can be your small group coach. Here are ten reasons to check out this website:

1. Top twenty questions every new leader asks
2. Common problems most new leaders face and ways to overcome them
3. Seven steps to building a healthy small group in six weeks
4. Free downloadable resources and leadership support
5. Additional leadership training material for every lesson in the EXPERIENCING CHRIST TOGETHER series
6. Ten stories from leaders who successfully completed this study
7. Free chat rooms and bulletin boards
8. Downloadable Health Assessments and Health Plans for individuals or groups
9. A chance to join a community of small group leaders by affinity, geography, or denominational affiliation
10. Best of all, a free newsletter with the best ideas from leaders around the world

LIFE TOGETHER AGREEMENT

OUR PURPOSE

To transform our spiritual lives by cultivating our spiritual health in a healthy small group community. In addition, we: _____

_____

_____.

OUR VALUES

Group Attendance	To give priority to the group meeting. We will call or email if we will be late or absent. (Completing the Small Group Calendar on page 76 will minimize this issue.)
Safe Environment	To help create a safe place where people can be heard and feel loved. (Please, no quick answers, snap judgments, or simple fixes.)
Respect Differences	To be gentle and gracious to people with different spiritual maturity, personal opinions, temperaments, or imperfections. We are all works in progress.
Confidentiality	To keep anything that is shared strictly confidential and within the group, and to avoid sharing improper information about those outside the group.
Encouragement for Growth	To be not just takers but givers of life. We want to spiritually multiply our life by serving others with our God-given gifts.
Welcome for Newcomers	To keep an open chair and share Jesus' dream of finding a shepherd for every sheep.
Shared Ownership	To remember that every member is a minister and to ensure that each attender will share a

small team role or responsibility over time. (See Team Roles on pages 77–79.)

Rotating Hosts/Leaders and Homes To encourage different people to host the group in their homes, and to rotate the responsibility of facilitating each meeting. (See the Small Group Calendar on page 76.)

OUR EXPECTATIONS

• Refreshments/mealtimes _____

• Child care _____

• When we will meet (day of week) _____

• Where we will meet (place) _____

• We will begin at (time)_____ and end at _____

• We will do our best to have some or all of us attend a worship service together. Our primary worship service time will be _____

• Date of this agreement _____

• Date we will review this agreement again _____

• Who (other than the leader) will review this agreement at the end of this study_____

SMALL GROUP CALENDAR

Planning and calendaring can help ensure the greatest participation at every meeting. At the end of each meeting, review this calendar. Be sure to include a regular rotation of host homes and leaders, and don't forget birthdays, socials, church events, holidays, and mission/ministry projects. Go to www.lifetogether.com for an electronic copy of this form and more than a hundred ideas for your group to do together.

Date	Lesson	Host Home	Dessert/Meal	Leader
Monday, January 15	1	Steve and Laura's	Joe	Bill

TEAM ROLES

The Bible makes clear that every member, not just the small group leader, is a minister in the body of Christ. In a healthy small group, every member takes on some small role or responsibility. It's more fun and effective if you team up on these roles.

Review the team roles and responsibilities below, and have each member volunteer for a role or participate on a team. If someone doesn't know where to serve or is holding back, have the group suggest a team or role. It's best to have one or two people on each team so you have each of the five purposes covered. Serving in even a small capacity will not only help your leader but also will make the group more fun for everyone. Don't hold back. Join a team!

The opportunities below are broken down by the five purposes and then by a *crawl* (beginning step), *walk* (intermediate step), or *run* (advanced step). Try to cover at least the crawl and walk roles, and select a role that matches your group, your gifts, and your maturity. If you can't find a good step or just want to see other ideas, go to www.lifetogether.com and see what other groups are choosing.

Team Roles	Team Player(s)
CONNECTING TEAM (Fellowship and Community Building)	
Crawl: Host a social event or group activity in the first week or two.	_____ _____
Walk: Create a list of uncommitted members and then invite them to an open house or group social.	_____ _____
Run: Plan a twenty-four-hour retreat or weekend getaway for the group. Lead the Connecting time each week for the group.	_____ _____

GROWING TEAM (Discipleship and Spiritual Growth)

Crawl: Coordinate the spiritual partners for the
group. Facilitate a three- or four-person
discussion circle during the Bible study
portion of your meeting. Coordinate the
discussion circles.

Walk: Tabulate the Personal Health Assessments
and Health Plans in a summary to let
people know how you're doing as a group.
Encourage personal devotions through group discussions
and pairing up with spiritual (accountability) partners.

Run: Take the group on a prayer walk, or plan
a day of solitude, fasting, or personal retreat.

SERVING TEAM (Discovering Your God-Given Design for Ministry)

Crawl: Ensure that every member finds a
group role or team he or she enjoys.

Walk: Have every member take a gift test
(see www.lifetogether.com) and
determine your group's gifts. Plan a
ministry project together.

Run: Help each member decide on a
way to use his or her unique gifts
somewhere in the church.

SHARING TEAM (Sharing and Evangelism)

Crawl: Coordinate the group's Prayer and
Praise Report of friends and family
who don't know Christ.

Walk: Search for group mission opportunities
and plan a cross-cultural group activity.

Run: Take a small-group "vacation" to host a
six-week group in your neighborhood
or office. Then come back together
with your current group.

SURRENDERING TEAM (Surrendering Your Heart to Worship)

Crawl: Maintain the group's Prayer
         and Praise Report or journal.   _____
                                                   _____

Walk: Lead a brief time of worship each   _____
         week (at the beginning or end of   _____
         your meeting), either a cappella or
         using a song from the DVD or the
         LIFE TOGETHER Worship DVD/CD.

Run: Plan a unique time of worship through   _____
         Communion, foot washing, night of   _____
         prayer, or nature walking.

PERSONAL HEALTH ASSESSMENT

	Just Beginning	Getting Going	Well Developed

CONNECTING WITH GOD AND OTHERS

I am deepening my understanding of and friendship
with God in community with others.   1 2 3 4 5

I am growing in my ability both to share and to
show my love to others.   1 2 3 4 5

I am willing to share my real needs for prayer and
support from others.   1 2 3 4 5

I am resolving conflict constructively and am
willing to forgive others.   1 2 3 4 5

CONNECTING Total _____

GROWING IN YOUR SPIRITUAL JOURNEY

I have a growing relationship with God through regular
time in the Bible and in prayer (spiritual habits).   1 2 3 4 5

I am experiencing more of the characteristics of
Jesus Christ (love, patience, gentleness, courage,
self-control, and so forth) in my life.   1 2 3 4 5

I am avoiding addictive behaviors (food, television,
busyness, and the like) to meet my needs.   1 2 3 4 5

I am spending time with a Christian friend (spiritual partner)
who celebrates and challenges my spiritual growth.   1 2 3 4 5

GROWING Total _____

SERVING WITH YOUR GOD-GIVEN DESIGN

I have discovered and am further developing my
unique God-given design.   1 2 3 4 5

I am regularly praying for God to show me
opportunities to serve him and others.   1 2 3 4 5

I am serving in a regular (once a month or more)
ministry in the church or community.   1 2 3 4 5

I am a team player in my small group by sharing
some group role or responsibility.   1 2 3 4 5

SERVING Total _____

SHARING GOD'S LOVE IN EVERYDAY LIFE

I am cultivating relationships with non-Christians and praying
for God to give me natural opportunities to share his love. 1 2 3 4 5

I am praying and learning about where God can use me
and my group cross-culturally for missions. 1 2 3 4 5

I am investing my time in another person or group who
needs to know Christ. 1 2 3 4 5

I am regularly inviting unchurched or unconnected
friends to my church or small group. 1 2 3 4 5

SHARING Total _____

SURRENDERING YOUR LIFE TO GOD

I am experiencing more of the presence and
power of God in my everyday life. 1 2 3 4 5

I am faithfully attending services and my
small group to worship God. 1 2 3 4 5

I am seeking to please God by surrendering every
area of my life (health, decisions, finances,
relationships, future, and the like) to him. 1 2 3 4 5

I am accepting the things I cannot change and
becoming increasingly grateful for the life I've been given. 1 2 3 4 5

SURRENDERING Total _____

Connecting Growing Serving Sharing Surrendering

20 — Well Developed
16 — Very Good
12 — Getting Going
8 — Fair
4 — Just Beginning

○ Beginning Assessment Total _____   ☐ Ending Assessment Total _____

PERSONAL HEALTH PLAN

This worksheet could become your single most important feature in this study. On it you can record your personal priorities before the Father. It will help you live a healthy spiritual life, balancing all five of God's purposes.

PURPOSE	PLAN
CONNECT	WHO are you connecting with spiritually?
GROW	WHAT is your next step for growth?
DEVELOP	WHERE are you serving?
SHARE	WHEN are you shepherding another in Christ?
SURRENDER	HOW are you surrendering your heart?

Additional copies of the Personal Health Plan may be downloaded in a larger format at www.lifetogether.com/healthplan.

DATE	MY PROGRESS	PARTNER'S PROGRESS

SAMPLE PERSONAL HEALTH PLAN

This worksheet could become your single most important feature in this study. On it you can record your personal priorities before the Father. It will help you live a healthy spiritual life, balancing all five of God's purposes.

PURPOSE	PLAN
CONNECT	WHO are you connecting with spiritually? *Bill and I will meet weekly by email or phone.*
GROW	WHAT is your next step for growth? *Regular devotions or journaling my prayers 2x/week*
DEVELOP	WHERE are you serving? *Serving in Children's Ministry* *Go through GIFTS class*
SHARE	WHEN are you shepherding another in Christ? *Shepherding Bill at lunch or hosting a starter group in the fall*
SURRENDER	HOW are you surrendering your heart? *Help with our teenager* *New job situation*

DATE	MY PROGRESS	PARTNER'S PROGRESS
3/5	Talked during our group	Figured out our goals together
3/12	Missed our time together	Missed our time together
3/26	Met for coffee and review of my goals	Met for coffee
4/10	Emailed prayer requests	Bill sent me his prayer requests
3/5	Great start on personal journaling	Read Mark 1–6 in one sitting!
3/12	Traveled and not doing well this week	Journaled about Christ as Healer
3/26	Back on track	Busy and distracted; asked for prayer
3/1	Need to call Children's Pastor	
3/26	Group did a serving project together	Agreed to lead group worship
3/30	Regularly rotating leadership	Led group worship—great job!
3/5	Called Jim to see if he's open to joining our group	Wanted to invite somebody, but didn't
3/12	Preparing to start a group this fall	
3/30	Group prayed for me	Told friend something he's learning about Christ
3/5	Overwhelmed but encouraged	Scared to lead worship
3/15	Felt heard and more settled	Issue with wife
3/30	Read book on teens	Glad he took on his fear

JOURNALING 101

Henri Nouwen says effective and lasting ministry *for* God grows out of a quiet place alone *with* God. This is why journaling is so important.

The greatest adventure of our lives is found in the daily pursuit of knowing, growing in, serving, sharing, and worshiping Christ forever. This is the essence of a purposeful life: to see all five biblical purposes fully formed and balanced in our lives. Only then are we "complete in Christ" (Colossians 1:28, NASB).

David poured his heart out to God by writing psalms. The book of Psalms contains many of his honest conversations with God in written form, including expressions of every imaginable emotion on every aspect of his life. Like David, we encourage you to select a strategy to integrate God's Word and journaling into your devotional time. Use any of the following resources:

- Bible
- One-year Bible
- New Testament Bible Challenge Reading Plan
  (www.lifetogether.com/readingprograms)
- Devotional book
- Topical Bible study plan

Before or after you read a portion of God's Word, speak to God in honest reflection or response in the form of a written prayer. You may begin this time by simply finishing the sentence "Father …," "Yesterday Lord …,"or "Thank you, God, for. …" Share with him where you are at the present moment; express your hurts, disappointments, frustrations, blessings, victories, gratefulness. Whatever you do with your journal, make a plan that fits you so you'll have a positive experience. Consider sharing highlights of your progress and experiences with some or all of your group members, especially your spiritual partner(s). You may find they want to join and even encourage you in this journey. Most of all, enjoy the ride and cultivate a more authentic, growing walk with God.

BIBLE READING PLAN

30 Days through the Gospel of John

Imagine sitting at the feet of Jesus himself: the Teacher who knows how to live life well, the Savior who died for you, the Lord who commands the universe. Like his first disciples, you can follow him around, watch what he does, listen to what he says, and pattern your life after his.

On the next page you will find a plan for reading through the gospel of John. Find a quiet place, and have ready a notebook or journal in which you can write what you learn and what you want to say back to God. You may also use the Reflections page at the end of each session of this study.

It's helpful to have one or two simple questions in mind to focus your reading. Here are some suggestions:

- What do I *learn* about Christ (his identity, personality, priorities)?

- How does he want me to *live* differently?

- What in this passage convinces me to entrust myself completely to Jesus?

- What about him moves me to worship?

When we've sat at the Master's feet like this ourselves, the sense of a real, alive, present Jesus has been breathtaking. We pray you'll have the same experience.

☐ Day 1   John 1:1–18
☐ Day 2   John 1:19–51
☐ Day 3   John 2:1–11
☐ Day 4   John 2:12–25
☐ Day 5   John 3:1–21
☐ Day 6   John 3:22–36
☐ Day 7   John 4
☐ Day 8   John 5:1–15
☐ Day 9   John 5:16–47
☐ Day 10 John 6:1–24
☐ Day 11 John 6:25–71
☐ Day 12 John 7:1–24
☐ Day 13 John 7:25–53
☐ Day 14 John 8:1–30
☐ Day 15 John 8:31–59

☐ Day 16 John 9
☐ Day 17 John 10
☐ Day 18 John 11
☐ Day 19 John 12
☐ Day 20 John 13
☐ Day 21 John 14:1–14
☐ Day 22 John 14:15–31
☐ Day 23 John 15:1–17
☐ Day 24 John 15:18–27
☐ Day 25 John 16
☐ Day 26 John 17
☐ Day 27 John 18
☐ Day 28 John 19
☐ Day 29 John 20
☐ Day 30 John 21

LEADING FOR
THE FIRST TIME

- **Sweaty palms are a healthy sign.** The Bible says God is gracious to the humble. Remember who is in control; the time to worry is when you're not worried. Those who are soft in heart (and sweaty-palmed) are those whom God is sure to speak through.

- **Seek support.** Ask your leader, coleader, or close friend to pray for you and prepare with you before the session. Walking through the study will help you anticipate potentially difficult questions and discussion topics.

- **Bring your uniqueness to the study.** Lean into who you are and how God wants you to uniquely lead the study.

- **Prepare. Prepare. Prepare.** Go through the session several times. If you are using the DVD, listen to the teaching segment and Leadership Lifter. Go to www.lifetogether.com and download pertinent files. Consider writing in a journal or fasting for a day to prepare yourself for what God wants to do.

- **Don't wait until the last minute to prepare.**

- **Ask for feedback so you can grow.** Perhaps in an email or on cards handed out at the study, have everyone write down three things you did well and one thing you could improve on. Don't get defensive, but show an openness to learn and grow.

- **Use online resources.** Go to www.lifetogether.com and listen to Brett Eastman share the weekly Leadership Lifter and download any additional notes or ideas for your session. You may also want to subscribe to the DOING LIFE TOGETHER Newsletter and LLT Newsletter. Both can be obtained for free by signing up at www.lifetogether.com/subscribe.

- **Prayerfully consider launching a new group.** This doesn't need to happen overnight, but God's heart is for this to happen over time. Not all

Christians are called to be leaders or teachers, but we are all called to be "shepherds" of a few someday.

- **Share with your group what God is doing in your heart.** God is searching for those whose hearts are fully his. Share your trials and victories. We promise that people will relate.

- **Prayerfully consider whom you would like to pass the baton to next week.** It's only fair. God is ready for the next member of your group to go on the faith journey you just traveled. Make it fun, and expect God to do the rest.

HOSTING AN OPEN HOUSE

If you're starting a new group, try planning an "open house" before your first formal group meeting. Even if you only have two to four core members, it's a great way to break the ice and to consider prayerfully who else might be open to join you over the next few weeks. You can also use this kick-off meeting to hand out study guides, spend some time getting to know each other, discuss each person's expectations for the group, and briefly pray for each other.

A simple meal or good desserts always make a kick-off meeting more fun. After people introduce themselves and share how they ended up being at the meeting (you can play a game to see who has the wildest story!), have everyone respond to a few icebreaker questions: "What is your favorite family vacation?" or "What is one thing you love about your church/our community?" or "What are three things about your life growing up that most people here don't know?" See www.lifetogether.com for more icebreaker ideas.

Next, ask everyone to tell what he or she hopes to get out of the study. You might want to review the LIFE TOGETHER Agreement (pages 74–75) and talk about each person's expectations and priorities.

Finally, set an open chair (maybe two) in the center of your group and explain that it represents someone who would enjoy or benefit from this group but who isn't here yet. Ask people to pray about whom they could invite to join the group over the next few weeks. Hand out postcards (see www.lifetogether.com for examples) and have everyone write an invitation or two. Don't worry about ending up with too many people—you can always have one discussion circle in the living room and another in the dining room after you watch the lesson. Each group could then report prayer requests and progress at the end of the session.

You can skip this kick-off meeting if your time is limited, but you'll experience a huge benefit if you take the time to connect with each other in this way.

EXPERIENCING CHRIST TOGETHER IN A SUNDAY SCHOOL SETTING

Sunday school is one of the best places to begin building community in your church, and the EXPERIENCING CHRIST TOGETHER DVDs and study guides work in concert to help your Sunday school leadership team do it easily and effectively.

Each study guide of the LIFE TOGETHER curriculum includes a companion DVD with today's top Christian leaders speaking to the passage of Scripture under discussion. Here is one way to use the DVD in a Sunday school class:

- Moderator introduction: welcome the class, and read the Scripture passage for the session
- DVD teaching segment: ten to fifteen minutes
- Small group discussion: divide into small groups of eight to twelve and, using the questions from the curriculum, discuss how the passage applies to each person in the class

So often Sunday school consists of the star teacher with little involvement from others. To use the EXPERIENCING CHRIST TOGETHER DVDs effectively means recruiting a host of people to participate in the Sunday school program. We recommend four teams:

Moderators. These are the facilitators or leaders of the class. Their role is to transition the class through each step in the time together. For example, the moderator will welcome the class and open with prayer. In addition, he or she will introduce the DVD segment by reading the Scripture passage for the session. We recommend that you recruit several moderaters. That allows you to rotate the moderators each week. Doing so takes the pressure off people to commit to every week of the class—and it offers more people opportunity for upfront leadership. One church recruited three sets of moderators (a total of six) because the Sunday school leaders wanted to use the curriculum for twelve weeks. They knew that out of twelve weeks, one set of moderators would, likely, burn out; it's difficult for anyone to provide leadership for twelve straight weeks.

Discussion Guides. These are people who lead the follow-up discussion after the DVD teaching segment. If, for example, your Sunday school runs for an hour, you may want to plan on fifteen to twenty minutes for the DVD teaching segment and an additional twenty to thirty minutes in small group discussion afterward. One church recruited many of its seniors to lead the discussion groups. Some of them had felt excluded from ministry, and the role of discussion guide opened the door for them to serve.

Each discussion guide needs only to read through the passage and the questions in each study guide for preparation. After the DVD teaching segment, the moderator of the class asks the discussion guides to stand up. Then, people circle their chairs around each discussion guide. It's an easy way to create small groups each week. You may need to help some groups find more people or other groups to divide once more, if they end up too large. One church asked some of the discussion guides to move their groups into different rooms, because the seniors had a hard time hearing.

Hospitality Coordinators. These are those who oversee the food and drink for the class. Some classes may not provide this, but for those who do, it's important that multiple people join the team, so one or two people don't burn out over the course of the class.

Technical Coordinators. There's nothing worse than a DVD player that doesn't seem to work. Recruit at least one person to oversee making sure the DVD works each week. It's best, though, to recruit two or three people, in order to rotate them throughout the Sunday school series. It's important that the technical team has made sure the DVD player works *before* the class begins.

One church decided to gather all the adult Sunday school classes together for a twelve-week series using the Life Together DVD and study guides. What happened was amazing—instead of Sunday school starting off with 140 people and ending up with half that many at the end of the fall, attendance stayed high the entire time. Instead of one Sunday school class being led by one or two teachers, more than thirty-five people were involved in some kind of leadership—as moderators, discussion guides, hospitality (food) coordinators, or technical coordinators. The fifteen-minute time at the beginning of Sunday school for coffee and snacks (fruit, coffee cake, etc.) proved just as valuable as the content portion!

The fall program gave the church a new vision for how Sunday school can support the larger issue of spiritual formation and life change. For more ideas and practical tools to strengthen your small group ministry, go to www.lifetogethertoday.com.

A SIMPLE
RETREAT PLAN

A retreat for your small group need not be complex or expensive. You don't need a large facility or a retreat speaker. In fact, the less outside stimulation, the better. The goal of the plan below is to give you downtime in which your minds and bodies are not occupied with learning information or doing tasks. This relatively empty time will allow you to hear the "gentle whisper" of the Lord, as did the prophet Elijah (1 Kings 19:12).

1. *Find a location.* A park or a room at your church would be adequate. If you know a family who will be away from home for a day, you could meet in their empty house. Don't use the home of someone who will be attending the retreat—one's own home tends to be full of distractions. Turn off the phones and put pets where they won't disturb you.

2. *Plan the schedule.* Here is a sample schedule for a half-day retreat:

9:00–9:30	Gather. Share some light breakfast food (coffee, tea, bagels, fruit) or picnic food. Socialize.
9:30–10:00	Worship. If you don't have access to electricity or a musician, you can read one or more psalms aloud together. Make photocopies of the psalm so that everyone has the same words. For a couples group, you could have men read the odd-numbered verses and women read the even-numbered ones. Some useful opening psalms are Psalms 136, 138, 145, and 148. Some more reflective psalms are Psalms 18 (you may shorten it), 25, 27, 131, and 139. Colossians 1:15–20 could also be used.
	If you have access to electricity and a CD or DVD player, use the LIFE TOGETHER DVD/CD Worship series or CDs of your choice. If people are unfamiliar with the songs, play a song once without singing, then play it again and let people sing. Have the volume at a level where people who don't want to be heard can sing quietly anyway. You might want to start with a couple of lively songs and then move to quieter ones.

10:00–11:00	Solitude and silence. If you're indoors and have only one room, simply let people move to different parts of the room. If you're outdoors or in a home, people can scatter more widely. Have each person bring a Bible, a journal or notebook, and a pen or pencil. Their task during this time is to soak in a small portion of God's Word and listen for what God is saying to their hearts. It's okay to meditate on just one verse for the whole hour. If their minds tend to wander, it may be helpful to write their thoughts and prayers about the verse(s). The goal is to listen closely to the words, to understand what they mean, to listen to any doubts they have about whether these words are really true for them, and to come to believe them deeply. Here are some passages to choose from:

☐ Psalm 23
☐ Isaiah 43:18–21
☐ Matthew 7:7–11
☐ Matthew 11:28–30
☐ Luke 12:27–31
☐ Colossians 3:1–3
☐ 1 Peter 2:1–10

An hour of solitude and silence is hard for many people. For those who are new to this, twenty minutes may be all they can handle. After that, it's okay for them to go for a walk or even sit back, shut their eyes, and doze. This is downtime, not do-time. The only rule is that they can't talk to anyone, read anything other than their short Bible passage, or turn on any entertainment.

11:00–11:30	Discuss this experience as a whole group. What was it like for you? What, if anything, did you sense God saying to you? What did you do? What did you think about? If you had trouble staying quiet, what was that like?
11:30–12:00	Worship and prayer aloud as a group.

3. *Supplies.* For the above retreat, the planners will need to provide: chairs or cushions for people to sit on; a few cushions for those who want

to lie back and shut their eyes during silent time (seriously, sometimes the most spiritual thing a person can do is rest); light breakfast food; a CD player and/or television for worship DVD. Individuals will need to bring a Bible, a journal or notebook, and a pen.

4. *Modification for a full-day retreat.* The above plan assumes you have three hours. If you have six hours, you can follow this schedule:

9:00–9:30	Food and social time.
9:30-10:00	Worship.
10:00–11:00	Solitude and silence.
11:00–11:30	Meet with your spiritual partner to share what you're hearing from God.
11:30–12:30	Lunch. (Provide this or ask participants to bring their own.) Eat lunch on-site in silence. Finish lunch by reading a psalm together.
12:30–1:00	Go for a walk alone.
1:00–1:45	Solitude and silence.
1:45–2:30	Debrief with group.
2:30–3:00	Worship and prayer.

INTRODUCTION

If your group is new, or even if you haven't been together for a few weeks, we recommend that you plan a kick-off meeting where you will pray, hand out study guides, spend some time getting to know each other, and discuss each person's expectations for the group. A meeting like this is a great way to start a group or step up people's commitments.

Most groups, if reconvened after a short break, will be renewed in seeing each other and open to increasing their commitment as much as 25 percent. We have seen some naturally move to a weekly format, begin doing homework, and commit to daily devotions simply because the leader shared his or her heart. What do you sense God wants from you and your group?

However, if your group is brand new, a simple meal, potluck, or even good desserts make a kick-off meeting more fun. After dessert, have everyone respond to an icebreaker question, such as, "How did you hear of this church, and what's one thing you love about it?" Or, "Tell us three things about your life growing up that most people here don't know."

Then ask everyone to tell what he or she hopes to get out of this study. You might want to review the LIFE TOGETHER Agreement (see pages 74–75) and talk about each person's expectations and priorities. You could discuss whether you want to do Bible study homework before each meeting—homework covering the questions under the Growing and/or the For Deeper Study sections. Review the Small Group Calendar on page 76 and talk about who else is willing to open their home or facilitate a meeting.

Finally, cast the vision, as Jesus did, to be inclusive not exclusive. Ask everyone to think of people who would enjoy or benefit from a group like this. The beginning of a new study is a great time to welcome a few people into your circle. Have each person share a name or two and either make phone calls the coming week or handwrite invitations or postcards that very night. This will make it fun and also make it happen. At www.lifetogether .com we have a free email invitation you may send to every potential member. Don't worry about ending up with too many people—you can always have one discussion circle in the living room and another in the dining room.

SESSION ONE: THE TREASURE OF DISCIPLESHIP

As a leader, your most important job is to create an atmosphere where people are willing to talk honestly about what Christ's words and actions have to do with them. Especially if your group is new, be available before people arrive so you can greet them at the door. People are naturally nervous at a new group, so a hug or handshake can help put them at ease.

You may ask a few people to come early to help set up, pray, and introduce newcomers to others. Even if everyone is new, they don't know that yet and may be shy when they arrive. You might give people roles like setting up nametags or handing out drinks. This could be a great way to spot a coleader.

Question 1. This question will help you get to know each other while beginning to think about the theme of this study: growth and change. You should be the first to answer this question while others are thinking about how to respond. Some people are embarrassed to say things they like about themselves, while others resist the idea of change. You can model a healthy self-assessment. Your level of depth will set the tone—you can be light-hearted (I'd like to change my waistline) or deep (I'd like to be warmer when I meet new people) depending on what you think best suits your group. Be sure to give everyone a chance to respond to this question, because it's a chance for the group to get to know each other. It's not necessary to go around the circle in order. Just ask for volunteers to respond.

Introduction to the Series. If this is your first LIFE TOGETHER study, take a moment after question 1 to orient the group to one principle that undergirds this series: *A healthy small group balances the purposes of the church.* Most small groups emphasize Bible study, fellowship, and prayer. But God has called us to reach out to others as well. He wants us to *do* what Jesus teaches, not just *learn about* it. You may spend less time in this series studying the Bible than some group members are used to. That's because you'll spend more time doing things the Bible says believers should do.

However, those who like more Bible study can find plenty of it in this series. At the end of each session, For Deeper Study provides more passages you can study on the same topic. If your group likes to do deeper Bible study, consider having members answer next week's Growing section questions ahead of time as homework. They can even study next week's For Deeper

Study passages for homework too. Then, during the Growing portion of your meeting, you can share the high points of what you've learned.

If the five biblical purposes are new to your group, be sure to review them together on pages 8–10 of the Read Me First section.

Question 2. An agreement helps you clarify your group's priorities and cast new vision for what the group can be. Members can imagine what your group could be like if they lived these values. So turn to pages 74–75 and choose one value that you want to emphasize in this study. We've suggested some options. If you choose "rotating leaders," you don't need to invest a lot of time in it now. In session 3 you'll have a chance to plan who will lead each meeting.

Question 3. Have someone read the Bible passage aloud. It's a good idea to ask someone ahead of time, because not everyone is comfortable reading aloud in public. When the passage has been read, ask question 3. *It is not necessary that everyone answer every question in the Bible study.* In fact, a group can become boring if you simply go around the circle and give answers. Your goal is to create a discussion—which means that perhaps only a few people respond to each question and an engaging dialogue gets going. It's even fine to skip some questions in order to spend more time on questions you believe are most important.

In this question, try to draw out the priceless qualities of God's kingdom, such as justice, beauty, truth, the chance to be who you were made to be, and intimacy with God himself.

Question 5. Read the study note for "bought." Grace means we don't earn our salvation. Yet we still need to put effort into our response to salvation. Among the costs of living as citizens of God's kingdom are time, energy, mental attention to God, and the risk of opposition from other people.

Question 6. The man is joyful because the value of what he bought exceeds the cost he paid. Jesus' point is that the value of the kingdom exceeds the cost God asks from us, even though that cost is everything we have. If paying the cost of discipleship doesn't bring us joy, it's because we don't fully comprehend the value of what we're getting.

Question 7. This question is crucial. Everyone in your group should leave this meeting with a vivid sense of the benefits of life in a kingdom where things are done God's way. If they don't deeply believe in the benefits, they aren't likely to sustain an interest in actually doing things God's way. Eternal salvation is an important benefit, but the benefits also include very practical things in this life: peace (Romans 8:6; Isaiah 26:3); hope, a strong character that can handle any suffering life brings, and an abiding sense that God loves us (Romans 5:1–5); wisdom for dealing with challenges (James 1:5–7); freedom from destructive habits (Romans 7:15–25); and richer relationships (James 3:13–4:3).

Question 8. Daily discipleship will cost us, at a minimum, time and the discomfort of change. Jesus wants to reshape our habits, and some habits die hard. But the cost of not undergoing this renovation is losing our selves. At best, we're left with a shrunken version of what we could be; at worst, we risk being saved "as one escaping through the flames" (1 Corinthians 3:15) with nothing to show for our lives when we stand before God.

Question 11. We've offered several options for personal time with God, which we consider essential for every believer. Walk the group through these options. If group members have never read the gospel of John, we strongly urge that they do so. This will immerse them in the person of Christ for the duration of this study. We also encourage them to write down what they discover on the Reflections page situated at the end of each session (or in a notebook).

Those who prefer topical Bible study might want to do the For Deeper Study section as homework each week. It's important that people know this study can adapt to a more spiritually mature group.

For those who have done a lot of Bible study, we encourage the meditation option. Living with one short passage each week can help people move biblical truth from their heads into their hearts and actions.

Question 12. One of the values of the LIFE TOGETHER agreement is "welcome for newcomers." Some groups fear that newcomers will interrupt the intimacy that members have built over time. However, groups generally gain strength with the infusion of new blood. It's like a river of living water flowing into a stagnant pond. Some groups remain permanently open, while others open periodically, such as at the beginning and ending of a study. Love grows by giving itself away. If your circle becomes too large for easy face-to-face conversations, you can simply form a second discussion circle in another room of your home.

As leader, you should do this exercise yourself in advance and be ready to share the names of the people you're going to invite or connect with. Your modeling is the number-one example people will follow. Give everyone a few moments in which to write down names before each shares. You might pray for a few of these names on the spot and/or later in the session. Encourage people not to be afraid to ask someone. Almost no one is annoyed to be invited to something! Most people are honored to be asked, even if they can't make it. You may want to hand out invitations and fill them out in the group. Check out the print and email invitations at www.lifetogether.com.

We encourage an outward focus for your group because groups that become too inwardly focused tend to become unhealthy over time. People naturally gravitate to feeding themselves through Bible study, prayer, and social time, so it's usually up to the leader to push them to consider how this inward nourishment can overflow into outward concern for others. Never forget: Jesus came to seek and save the lost and to find a shepherd for every sheep.

Question 15. Never pressure a person to pray aloud. That's a sure way to scare someone away from your group. So instead of praying in a circle (which makes it obvious when someone stays silent), allow open time when anyone can pray who wishes to. Have someone write down everyone's prayer requests on the Prayer and Praise Report (page 21). If your time is short, consider having people share requests and pray just with their spiritual partners or in smaller circles of three or four.

As you begin, welcome any new people and praise the ones who brought them. Renew the vision to welcome people for one more week and model this if you can.

Then have everyone sit back, relax, close their eyes, and listen to one of the songs on the DVD or LIFE TOGETHER Worship DVD/CD series. You may want to sing the second time through as a group, or simply be silent for a few moments to focus on God and transition from the distractions of your day.

If newcomers have joined you, take a few minutes before the Grow section to let all members introduce themselves. The first visit to a new group is scary, so be sure to minimize the inside jokes. Introduce newcomers to some highly relational people when they arrive and partner them with great spiritual partners to welcome them to their first meeting.

We highly recommend that as leader, you read the Study Notes ahead of time and draw the group's attention to anything there that will help them understand the Bible passage.

Question 2. This desert time is more noteworthy for what Jesus didn't do than for what he did. He didn't eat and he didn't give in to the Devil's temptations. With no books or other media, he didn't have a lot to stimulate or distract him. He probably didn't "do" much. All that silence and solitude left him lots of time to think, pray, listen to his Father, and confront temptations. That may seem relaxing, but it probably wasn't. We generally like to be busy, even at events we call "retreats." It's scary when the Holy Spirit strips down our lives and we're alone with nothing to do and no one except ourselves, God, and the tempter. We're vulnerable.

Question 3. The first temptation may be interpreted in various ways. Perhaps the Devil wanted Jesus to stay tethered to his body's survival instincts, putting his physical needs ahead of the Father's agenda. It's hard to follow God's call when our own needs come first. Or perhaps the Devil wanted Jesus to see his mission purely as providing people with physical bread. As important as it is to meet others' physical needs, that wasn't Jesus' most important mission. In the second temptation, the Devil offered Jesus worldly power. Ironically, in the second and third temptations he offered to give Jesus something quickly and easily (by worshiping Satan) that Jesus would eventually get the hard way (by going through crucifixion). The Father did eventually rescue Jesus from death, and Scripture tells us that the resurrected Jesus has all authority and splendor (Matthew 28:18; Philippians 2:9–11; Revelation 5:9–14).

Question 5. Jesus needed to face the things that would be most attractive to him when his ministry got tough. He needed to know his areas of vulnerability and know how to resist them. This time of temptation prepared him for situations when people would try to make him a celebrity or would ask him to work miracles for trivial reasons. Resisting temptation makes us stronger the next time; giving in makes us weaker the next time.

Question 6. We tend to be driven by our desires and by the demands of our bodies. Fasting exposes our drivenness by denying those desires and demands. Just as solitude forces us to deal with the inner voices we try to drown out most of the time, fasting forces us to deal with our insatiable hungers. We are reduced to dependence on God.

Question 9. God's Word concerning what is true and right, about what's important in life, has divine power against the enemy's lies and temptations (Ephesians 6:10–18).

Question 12. For those who haven't done a LIFE TOGETHER study before, spiritual partners will be a new idea. We highly encourage you to try pairs or triplets for six weeks. It's so hard to start a spiritual practice like prayer or consistent Bible reading with no support. A friend makes a huge difference. Partners can check in with each other weekly either at the beginning of your group meetings or outside the meeting.

Question 14. Be sure to save time to pray for those who are going through desert times. Sometimes people just feel dry inside and don't know why. Avoid the temptation to fix people's problems. Instead, allow them to tell what they're feeling, and then pray for them. Holding hands or placing your hand on the person's shoulder is a great way to communicate that you care.

SESSION THREE: PRESSING THE PAUSE BUTTON

In order to maximize your time together and honor the diversity of personality types, do your best to begin and end your group on time. You may even want to adjust your starting or stopping time. Don't hesitate to open in prayer even before everyone is seated. This isn't disrespectful of those who are still gathering—it respects those who are ready to begin, and the others won't be offended. An opening prayer can be as simple as, "Welcome, Lord! Help us! Now let's start."

If you've had trouble getting through all of the Bible study questions, consider breaking into smaller circles of four or five people for the Bible study (Growing) portion of your meeting. Everyone will get more "airtime," and the people who tend to dominate the discussion will be balanced out. A circle of four doesn't need an experienced leader, and it's a great way to identify and train a coleader.

Questions 1 and 2. Checking in with your spiritual partners (question 2) will be an option in all sessions from now on. You'll need to watch the clock and keep these conversations to ten minutes. If partners want more time together (as is ideal), they can connect before, after, or outside meetings. Give them a two-minute notice and hold to it if you ever want to get them back in the circle! If some group members are absent or newcomers have joined you, you may need to help partnerless people connect with new or temporary partners.

If you prefer (and especially if there are many newcomers), question 1 will always be a lighter icebreaker for the whole group. We encourage you, though, to let partners check in at least every other week so that those relationships grow solid. Please don't miss this opportunity to take your people deeper. Remember that the goal here is "transforming lives through community," and one-on-one time has an enormous return on time spent. In a week or two, you might want to ask the group how their partnerships are going and what kind of progress is being made. This will encourage those who are struggling to connect or accomplish their goals.

Question 3. Remember that your group may become boring if you let every group member answer a question like this one. Two or three responses for each Bible passage are plenty. Also remember that if people are silent before they answer, it's because they're thinking!

Question 4. We tend to think it was effortless for Jesus to prioritize his life, manage his stress, govern his emotions, and treat every person with love because he was both divine and sinless. But he was fully human, and he practiced habits that helped him stay focused and fueled instead of scattered and drained. Periods of solitude, silence, and prayer helped him. Intense intimacy with the Father enabled him to see what the Father was doing around him, and he focused his energy there (John 5:19). Also, Jesus chose not to be driven by others' expectations, even when they pressured him (John 7:1–9). Solitude gave him the emotional and spiritual fuel for ministry.

Question 9. We need to become convinced that the benefits of taking time alone outweigh the costs. Because our world rewards us for being productive, we need to see the spiritual rewards of solitude. We can actually love people better when we've taken time to relax in God's presence and become full of his love for us.

Question 13. You'll be amazed at the growth you'll see in individuals and in your connections as a group if you have at least a half-day retreat. It's not difficult to plan a simple retreat because the priority is not to plan activities but to give people time and space to do nothing in God's presence. Doing nothing with God is highly productive, as Jesus' time in the desert attests.

You should not shoulder the job of planning the retreat. If no one volunteers to plan it, don't be discouraged. Who do you think are the one or two party people in your group? They are likely to respond well if you ask them right after your meeting to take on this project and if you ask two people to team up. Another surefire approach is to ask the group which two group members are perfect for this task.

You may well hear people complaining they're too busy for a retreat. That's exactly why they need one! If you are committed to scheduling retreat time, others will follow your example.

SESSION FOUR:
PERSISTENT PRAYER

Question 1. If you decide to discuss this question, you as leader should go first with a brief and honest response. This session is about asking the Father for what we need, and one of the main reasons people struggle with this is that experience has led them to expect disappointment when they ask. Your group may well include a few people who had very troubled experiences with parents. Thank them for being honest with the group about that, and ask them to keep their past experience in mind as they reflect on the Bible passage.

Question 3. God is at the same time our intimate Dad and utterly holy. He's both as close as our breath and far beyond us. It's hard to keep both of those truths in mind at once. We often drift into thinking of him as our distant Dad, especially if our earthly fathers were distant. Jesus' parables later in this passage are designed to shake up this misconception of God as distant and uncaring.

Also, God is our provider. He is the One whom our sins grieve most, but he's eager to forgive. God never tempts us to do wrong (James 1:13–18), but just as he sent Jesus into the desert where he'd be vulnerable to temptation, so he sometimes sends us into situations where we'll be vulnerable. Yet he's eager to respond to our prayers for protection and deliverance.

Question 4. In the story, the man is motivated not by friendship but by his neighbor's "boldness"—his neighbor persists because rejection doesn't scare him and he really needs the bread. If even a self-centered man can be motivated by our boldness, how much more will the God who loves us respond to bold, persistent pleas.

Question 8. It's very important to make your group a safe place for people to admit the ways in which they feel God has let them down. God is utterly good, but he doesn't need us to defend him. People who have been through suffering often struggle with trusting God, and it helps them when we give them time to express their mistrust. Don't try to argue them into agreeing that God is good and their suffering was for the best. Instead, listen to them and then pray lovingly for them.

Question 10. It's entirely appropriate to pray for concrete things like a job or a house. But often what we most need are the things the Holy Spirit provides: wisdom, guidance, joy, peace, self-control, the ability to tell right from wrong, an accurate perception of our Father, a deeper capacity to love difficult people, and so on.

Question 11. Please do this exercise as a model for your group, and come back next week ready to tell them honestly how it went.

Question 13. As leader, you're in the people development business. Part of your job is to help others discover and develop their gifts. You may not need their help to plan a retreat or lead a meeting, but they need you to let them take on a role and support them so that they succeed. If you have children, you know that it's often easier to do a job yourself than to help someone else learn to do it. But that's what Jesus did with his disciples, and it's what he wants us to do for those we lead.

So if your group has already experimented with small responsibilities, urge them to move on to create purpose teams for sixty days. Beginners can do the crawl steps, while more mature group members should tackle the walk or run steps. Especially if you have members who want more Bible study to dig deeper, this is a chance to motivate them to be doers of God's Word.

SESSION FIVE: BUILDING ON A SOLID FOUNDATION

Question 3. Our culture highly values independence, the freedom to do as we please. We are suspicious of authority and are more interested in rights than responsibilities. We have seen powerful people abuse their power, and we may even have been abused by authority figures when we were young. It's hard for us to imagine that doing things somebody else's way (God's way) could ultimately make us happier and more fulfilled than doing them the way we want. It's even harder for us to imagine that somebody else (God) has the right to tell us what to do because he made us. We think a loving God would want to help us get our way.

Question 4. We might say we don't understand what Jesus is telling us to do. In a franker moment we might admit that we're uncomfortable with his instructions because they go against the grain of our habits or because they cost us things we value (money, time, status, emotional or physical safety).

Question 6. It's very important for people to understand that storms are standard in life, and God nowhere promises to exempt us. In his parable, Jesus promises to equip us to deal with storms because they are inevitable in a fallen world.

Question 8. The unsettling fact is that doing good to those who hate us will not necessarily put food on the table. It got Jesus killed, and it could get us killed. We might think getting killed is equivalent to, or even worse than, having the foundation of our life collapse. But Jesus doesn't see it that way. He thinks that dying for the right reasons keeps our life's foundation intact. He has an eternal perspective. We too need an eternal perspective in order to understand where our long-term best interests lie.

Question 10. Doing good to those who hate you is a risk. It becomes a reasonable risk only when you know that even if the worst happens, God will make sure you survive and flourish—if not in this life then eternally.

Question 11. You'll need to check in on the retreat every week to make sure progress is being made. People do what a leader inspects. These check-ins let them know you think the retreat is important.

Question 13. In session 2 you prayed for people in deserts. Now you're praying for people facing storms. These could be some of the same people. People often feel that God has abandoned them in their suffering. To some extent, *you* are what God is doing about their suffering. Your group is Christ in the flesh.

One final thing to do in this session is to confirm the group's interest in continuing to another study in this series. Show them the next study guide and collect the money in advance or have them pay you later.

SESSION SIX: WHERE'S YOUR TREASURE?

Whether your group is ending or continuing, it's important to celebrate where you've come together. Thank everyone for what they've contributed to the group. You might even give some thought ahead of time to something unique each person has contributed. You can say those things at the beginning of your meeting.

Question 3. Money and possessions are impermanent; they can be stolen or destroyed. Treasure in heaven is permanent and therefore reliable. This is hard for us to grasp because we can see and touch possessions, while treasure in heaven seems abstract and therefore less reliable. Furthermore, money has an alluring power that can easily master us if we're not actively choosing to serve God as our master. We often think money is a tool, when it's really a force with a power of its own.

Question 5. It might be helpful if you briefly share one thing you worry about. Also, it might be helpful to clarify that worry takes many forms. Some people are openly anxious. Others are driven. People who think they never worry but spend sixty hours a week at the office are deceiving themselves. They are highly concerned about something: perhaps making more money, maintaining their status, or keeping their job. The inability to rest is a sign of worry.

Question 6. People serve money because it buys so much of what we desire. Food and clothes were on the minds of Jesus' original audience, but to that list we might add physical attractiveness, sex, pain relief, entertainment, a comfortable home in a good neighborhood, people's approval, children's health care, education to get a good job, and many other things.

The problem isn't that we need things—food, warmth, sleep, health. The problem isn't that our children need things. God made us with needs. The problem comes when earthly desires (even for basic needs) become the focus of our lives.

Question 7. We don't need to worry about the things we desire because God can be trusted to provide what we need. One of the most useful spiritual things we can do is to sort out which of our desires are needs and which are merely desires. There's nothing wrong with desiring things we don't need, as long as we keep such desires in perspective. We can't allow them to run our lives.

ABOUT THE AUTHORS

The authors' previous work as a team includes the DOING LIFE TOGETHER Bible study series, which won a Silver Medallion from the Evangelical Christian Publishers Association, as well as the DOING LIFE TOGETHER DVD series.

Brett Eastman has served as the champion of Small Groups and Leadership Development for both Willow Creek Community Church and Saddleback Valley Community Church. Brett is now the Founder and CEO of Lifetogether, a ministry whose mission is to "transform lives through community." Brett earned his Masters of Divinity degree from Talbot School of Theology and his Management Certificate from Kellogg School of Business at Northwestern University. **Dee Eastman** is the real hero in the family, who, after giving birth to Joshua and Breanna, gave birth to identical triplets—Meagan, Melody, and Michelle. They live in Las Flores, California.

Todd and Denise Wendorff serve at King's Harbor Church in Redondo Beach, California. Todd is a teaching pastor, handles leadership development, and pastors men. He is also coauthor of the Every Man Bible Study Series. Denise speaks to women at conferences, classes, and special events. She also serves women through personal discipleship. Previously, Todd was on the pastoral staff at Harvest Bible Chapel, Willow Creek Community Church, and Saddleback Valley Community Church. He holds a Th.M. from Talbot School of Theology. Todd and Denise live in Rolling Hills Estates, California with their three children, Brooke, Brittany, and Brandon.

Karen Lee-Thorp has written or cowritten more than fifty books and Bible studies, including *How to Ask Great Questions* and *Why Beauty Matters*. Her previous Silver Medallion winners are *The Story of Stories*, *LifeChange: Ephesians*, and *LifeChange: Revelation*. She was a senior editor at NavPress for many years and series editor for the LifeChange Bible study series. She is now a freelance writer, speaks at women's retreats, and trains small group leaders. She lives in Brea, California, with her husband, Greg Herr, and their daughters, Megan and Marissa.

SMALL GROUP ROSTER

Name	Address	Phone	Email Address	Team or Role	Church Ministry
Bill Jones	7 Alvalar Street L.F. 92665	766-2255	bjones@aol.com	socials	children's ministry

(Pass your book around your group at your first meeting to get everyone's name and contact information.)

Name	Address	Phone	Email Address	Team or Role	Church Ministry

Experiencing Christ Together:
Living with Purpose in Community
Brett & Dee Eastman; Todd & Denise Wendorff;
Karen Lee-Thorp

Experiencing Christ Together: Living with Purpose in Community is a series of six, six-week study guides that offers small groups a chance to explore Jesus' teaching on the five biblical purposes of the church. By closely examining Christ's life and teaching in the Gospels, the series helps group members walk in the steps of Christ's early followers. Jesus lived every moment following God's purposes for his life, and Experiencing Christ Together helps groups learn how they can do this too. The first book lays the foundation: who Christ is and what he has done for us. Each of the other five books in the series looks at how Jesus trained his followers to live one of the five biblical purposes (fellowship, discipleship, service, evangelism, and worship).

	Softcovers	DVD
Beginning in Christ Together	ISBN: 0-310-24986-4	ISBN: 0-310-26187-2
Connecting in Christ Together	ISBN: 0-310-24981-3	ISBN: 0-310-26189-9
Growing in Christ Together	ISBN: 0-310-24985-6	ISBN: 0-310-26192-9
Serving Like Christ Together	ISBN: 0-310-24984-8	ISBN: 0-310-26194-5
Sharing Christ Together	ISBN: 0-310-24983-X	ISBN: 0-310-26196-1
Surrendering to Christ Together	ISBN: 0-310-24982-1	ISBN: 0-310-26198-8

Pick up a copy today at your favorite bookstore!

ZONDERVAN™

GRAND RAPIDS, MICHIGAN 49530 USA

WWW.ZONDERVAN.COM

life**together**.com

Beginning in Christ Together
Brett & Dee Eastman; Todd & Denise Wendorff; Karen Lee-Thorp

Beginning in Christ Together allows you to get to know Jesus as his first followers did. They met him as Teacher, a rabbi. They came to know him as Healer, Shepherd, Servant, Savior, and ultimately Risen Lord. From his first words, "follow me," through his ministry, death, and resurrection, he kept drawing them deeper into his life.

Experiencing Christ Together: Living with Purpose in Community is a series of six, six-week study guides that offers small groups a chance to explore Jesus' teaching on the five biblical purposes of the church. *Beginning in Christ Together*, the first book, lays the foundation: who Christ is and what he has done for us. Each of the other five books in the series looks at how Jesus trained his followers to live one of the five biblical purposes (fellowship, discipleship, service, evangelism, and worship).

Softcover: 0-310-24986-4
DVD: 0-310-26187-2

Pick up a copy today at your favorite bookstore!

GRAND RAPIDS, MICHIGAN 49530 USA

WWW.ZONDERVAN.COM

Connecting in Christ Together

Brett & Dee Eastman; Todd &
Denise Wendorff; Karen Lee-Thorp

Today, love is not always the first thing that
springs to mind when unbelievers think about
Christians. But it should be. Our mandate from
Jesus is simple: "Love one another as I have loved
you." What Christians call "fellowship" is one of God's core dreams for
his people. It's simply love, passionate and practical. If you need more
of that in your life and your group, study *Connecting in Christ Together*
and let Jesus show you how.

Experiencing Christ Together: Living with Purpose in Community is
a series of six, six-week study guides that offers small groups a chance
to explore Jesus' teaching on the five biblical purposes of the church.
The first book lays the foundation: who Christ is and what he has done
for us. Each of the other five books in the series, including this one, looks
at how Jesus trained his followers to live one of the five biblical purposes (fellowship, discipleship, service, evangelism, and worship).

Softcover: 0-310-24981-3
DVD: 0-310-26189-9

Pick up a copy today at your favorite bookstore!

ZONDERVAN™

GRAND RAPIDS, MICHIGAN 49530 USA

WWW.ZONDERVAN.COM

lifetogether.com

Growing in Christ Together
Brett & Dee Eastman; Todd &
Denise Wendorff; Karen Lee-Thorp

Jesus was the most remarkable rabbi of his day.
He is also the most remarkable rabbi of our day,
for he's still alive. If we're willing to be his followers, we can learn to do life the way Jesus
would if he had our temperaments, our families,
and our jobs. *Growing in Christ Together* can
help us to get our priorities in order.

Experiencing Christ Together: Living with Purpose in Community is
a series of six, six-week study guides that offers small groups a chance
to explore Jesus' teaching on the five biblical purposes of the church.
The first book lays the foundation: who Christ is and what he has done
for us. Each of the other five books in the series, including this one, looks
at how Jesus trained his followers to live one of the five biblical purposes (fellowship, discipleship, service, evangelism, and worship).

Softcover: 0-310-24985-6
DVD: 0-310-26192-9

Pick up a copy today at your favorite bookstore!

ZONDERVAN™

GRAND RAPIDS, MICHIGAN 49530 USA

WWW.ZONDERVAN.COM

life**together**.com

Serving Like Christ Together
Brett & Dee Eastman; Todd &
Denise Wendorff; Karen Lee-Thorp

Serviced shouldn't be something we force ourselves to do because we'll be punished if we
don't. It should flow from a heart formed as
Christ's is, by a passion for something greater
than ourselves. *Serving Like Christ Together*
investigates six qualities of a servant's heart that
Jesus highly valued.

Experiencing Christ Together: Living with Purpose in Community is
a series of six, six-week study guides that offers small groups a chance
to explore Jesus' teaching on the five biblical purposes of the church.
The first book lays the foundation: who Christ is and what he has done
for us. Each of the other five books in the series, including this one, looks
at how Jesus trained his followers to live one of the five biblical purposes (fellowship, discipleship, service, evangelism, and worship).

Softcover: 0-310-24984-8
DVD: 0-310-26194-5

Pick up a copy today at your favorite bookstore!

ZONDERVAN™

GRAND RAPIDS, MICHIGAN 49530 USA

W W W . Z O N D E R V A N . C O M

life**together**.com

Sharing Christ Together
Brett & Dee Eastman; Todd & Denise Wendorff; Karen Lee-Thorp

Jesus asks us to do what he did: help lost people learn how to navigate through life and find their Home. It doesn't matter than our map-reading skills aren't perfect yet. As long as we know a little more than someone else, we can gently and respectfully offer help. *Sharing Christ Together* will help you to do three things: develop your compassion for lost people, learn some useful sharing skills, and team up with a group to build relationships among the lost.

Experiencing Christ Together: Living with Purpose in Community is a series of six, six-week study guides that offers small groups a chance to explore Jesus' teaching on the five biblical purposes of the church. The first book lays the foundation: who Christ is and what he has done for us. Each of the other five books in the series, including this one, looks at how Jesus trained his followers to live one of the five biblical purposes (fellowship, discipleship, service, evangelism, and worship).

Softcover: 0-310-24983-X
DVD: 0-310-26196-1

Pick up a copy today at your favorite bookstore!

GRAND RAPIDS, MICHIGAN 49530 USA
WWW.ZONDERVAN.COM

Surrendering to Christ Together

Brett & Dee Eastman; Todd &
Denise Wendorff; Karen Lee-Thorp

In *Surrendering to Christ Together*, you'll inves-
tigate six heart attitudes that can motivate you
to totally abandon yourself to God's agenda. If
you've been holding back something from God
for fear of failure or loss, or because you're too busy pursuing your own
goals, take a good look at what motivated Jesus and his closest friends.

Experiencing Christ Together: Living with Purpose in Community is
a series of six, six-week study guides that offers small groups a chance
to explore Jesus' teaching on the five biblical purposes of the church.
The first book lays the foundation: who Christ is and what he has done
for us. Each of the other five books in the series, including this one, looks
at how Jesus trained his followers to live one of the five biblical purposes (fellowship, discipleship, service, evangelism, and worship).

Softcover: 0-310-24982-1
DVD: 0-310-26198-8

Pick up a copy today at your favorite bookstore!

GRAND RAPIDS, MICHIGAN 49530 USA

WWW.ZONDERVAN.COM

Doing Life Together series

Brett & Dee Eastman; Todd & Denise Wendorff;
Karen Lee-Thorp

Based on the five biblical purposes that form the bedrock of Saddleback Church, Doing Life Together will help your group discover what God created you for and how you can turn this dream into an everyday reality. Experience the transformation firsthand as you begin Connecting, Growing, Developing, Sharing, and Surrendering your life together for him.

"Doing Life Together is a groundbreaking study ... [It's] the first small group curriculum built completely on the purpose-driven paradigm ... The greatest reason I'm excited about [it] is that I've seen the dramatic changes it produces in the lives of those who study it."
—FROM THE FOREWORD BY RICK WARREN

Small Group Ministry Consultation

Building a healthy, vibrant, and growing small group ministry is challenging. That's why Brett Eastman and a team of certified coaches are offering small group ministry consultation. Join pastors and church leaders from around the country to discover new ways to launch and lead a healthy Purpose-Driven small group ministry in your church. To find out more information please call 1-800-467-1977.

	Softcover
Beginning Life Together	ISBN: 0-310-24672-5
Connecting with God's Family	ISBN: 0-310-24673-3
Growing to Be Like Christ	ISBN: 0-310-24674-1
Developing Your SHAPE to Serve Others	ISBN: 0-310-24675-X
Sharing Your Life Mission Every Day	ISBN: 0-310-24676-8
Surrendering Your Life for God's Pleasure	ISBN: 0-310-24677-6
Curriculum Kit	ISBN: 0-310-25002-1

ZONDERVAN™

GRAND RAPIDS, MICHIGAN 49530 USA

WWW.ZONDERVAN.COM

life**together**.com

Doing Life Together DVD series
Brett & Dee Eastman; Todd & Denise Wendorff;
Karen Lee-Thorp

The Doing Life Together series on DVD provides small group members with basic training on how to live healthy and balanced lives—purpose driven lives. Each DVD features practical techniques for leading small groups; a personal story, interview, drama, or music video related to the weekly topic; dynamic teaching featuring well-known teachers such as Bruce Wilkinson, John Ortberg, Carol Kent, Joe Stowell, and Erwin McManus; and worship music featuring the songs of Maranatha!

Based on the five biblical purposes that form the bedrock of Saddleback Church, Doing Life Together is a comprehensive study of the Purpose-Driven® Life. It will help you cultivate a healthy, balanced Christian life together with a friend, small group, or even your entire church. This experienced team of writers will take you on a spiritual journey, discovering not only what God created you for but also how you can turn that dream into an everyday reality. Experience the transformation firsthand as you Begin, Connect, Grow, Develop, Share, and Surrender your life together for him.

DVDs
Beginning Life Together   ISBN: 0-310-25004-8
Connecting with God's Family   ISBN: 0-310-25005-6
Growing to Be Like Christ   ISBN: 0-310-25006-4
Developing Your SHAPE to Serve Others   ISBN: 0-310-25007-2
Sharing Your Life Mission Every Day   ISBN: 0-310-25008-0
Surrendering Your Life for God's Pleasure   ISBN: 0-310-25009-9

Also available:
Boxed kit of 6 books and 6 DVDs   ISBN: 0-310-25002-1

Pick up a copy today at your favorite bookstore!

ZONDERVAN™
GRAND RAPIDS, MICHIGAN 49530 USA
WWW.ZONDERVAN.COM

lifetogether.com

Life Together Student Edition
Brett Eastman & Doug Fields

The Life Together series is the beginning of a relational journey, from being a member of a group to being a vital part of an unbelievable spiritual community. These books will help you think, talk, dig deep, care, heal, share . . . and have the time of your life! Life . . . together!

The Life Together Student Edition DVD Curriculum combines DVD teaching from well-known youth Bible teachers, as well as leadership training, with the Life Together Student Edition Small Group Series to give a new way to do small group study and ministry with basic training on how to live healthy and balanced lives-purpose driven lives.

Thirty-six sessions are included in the six-book curriculum:

STARTING to Go Where God Wants You to Be: 6 Small Group
    Sessions on Beginning
CONNECTING Your Hearts to Others: 6 Small Group Sessions
    on Fellowship
GROWING to Be Like Jesus: 6 Small Group Sessions on
    Discipleship
SERVING Others in Love: 6 Small Group Sessions on Ministry
SHARING Your Story and God's Story: 6 Small Group Sessions
    on Evangelism
SURRENDERING Your Life to Honor God: 6 Small Group
    Sessions on Worship

Teaching about the session's core Bible passage and theme, the lesson material takes the burden of correct interpretation off the leader, so less experienced leaders can be confident that their groups' direction stays biblically sound.

The kit includes 6 guides and 3 DVDs with inserts for leaders. Also available are the 6 student editions of the Doing Life Together Bible studies.

0-310-25339-X

 0-310-25340-3

0-310-25341-1

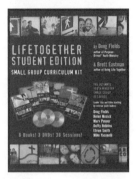 0-310-25332-2

0-310-25333-0

0-310-25334-9

0-310-25335-7

0-310-25336-5

0-310-25337-3

0-310-25338-1

We want to hear from you. Please send your comments about this book to us in care of zreview@zondervan.com. Thank you.

GRAND RAPIDS, MICHIGAN 49530 USA

WWW.ZONDERVAN.COM